BUSINESS LETTERS
THAT GET
RESULTS!

BUSINESS LETTERS
THAT GET
RESULTS!

J. HAMILTON JONES

BOB ADAMS, INC.
PUBLISHERS

Published by Bob Adams, Inc.
260 Center Street, Holbrook, MA 02343

ISBN: 1-55850-042-1

Printed in the United States of America

D   E   F   G   H   I   J

This book is available at quantity discounts for bulk purchases.
For information, call 1-800-872-5627.

CONTENTS

INTRODUCTION

Business Letters That Get Results will make a significant difference in your self-confidence, your promotability, and your job effectiveness. You'll be exposed to a wealth of new ideas that make your writing more productive and fun. You'll learn how to challenge today's traditional, stuffy letter and make your letters really stand out. And you'll find original techniques that give you an edge in your writing style.

Because the book's ideas are unique, I make these guarantees:

1. You'll discover revolutionary ideas you've never seen before.

2. You'll increase your effectiveness by using the ideas.

3. You'll be able to put the ideas to work immediately.

First, let's discuss the revolutionary ideas. My approach challenges the way we currently write letters. I don't like traditional salutations like "Dear Mr. Jones," "Ladies and Gentlemen," or "To Whom It May Concern." I don't like traditional complimentary closes like "Sincerely," "Yours truly," or "Cordially." They're stuffy, boring, and unimaginative.

Think about it. What do these traditional salutations and complimentary closes add to business letters? Do they add color or personality? Do they reinforce behavior? Do they add to the selling effort?

Definitely not! I say the traditional salutation and complimentary close are old-fashioned and add nothing to letters. They're like taking a buggy whip to a car and trying to get the car to go. Guess what? The buggy whip doesn't produce. Neither do formal salutations and complimentary closes. So why do we use them? Tradition.

Unfortunately, no one has challenged that tradition. I do in *Business Letters That Get Results*. I say use creative substitutions and replace today's formal language with creative language that lets you write the way you talk.

What is the creative substitution? It's a thought or message that replaces the traditional way we write salutations and complimentary closes. It's revolutionary, so let me explain.

Let's first replace a traditional salutation like "Dear Mr. Brown" in a friendly business letter. We might then use a creative substitution like "YOUR IDEA IS TERRIFIC, MR. BROWN." Notice that the creative substitution immediately improves the letter's tone. Who among us wouldn't want to continue reading if we received that letter?

Now let's replace a traditional complimentary close like "Yours truly" in a sales letter. Here we could use a creative substitution like "EXPECT RESULTS." This replacement not only stands out, but it gives us an ending selling message that strengthens the entire letter.

As you read the chapters in *Business Letters That Get Results,* you'll learn how to use creative substitution and why it works. In addition, you'll learn other unique ideas like how to create sales letters that stand out with customers, how to make complaint letters succeed, how to make *thank you* a tool that screams opportunity, and why *I'm sorry* should never appear in any letter.

My second guarantee says you'll improve your effectiveness. This is easy to understand, because the traditional salutation and complimentary close contribute to *ineffectiveness.* They don't make you stand out, and they certainly never differentiate you or your company from the competition.

But to gain market share, to get that marketing edge, to stand above the crowd, you must be especially good at differentiating. Creative substitutions help you with that difference. Let me explain with some examples.

Let's say your salutation's creative substitution reads, "IT MAKES A DIFFERENCE, MS. SMITH." With that creative substitution you instantly have a more powerful letter. You immediately grab attention, create an element of suspense with "IT," and focus your message by showing why "IT" makes a difference to the customer.

In effect, you've made it easier for the customer to read your letter and discover why you make a difference. And that's why we write letters in the first place—to have others read them.

Now let's replace the traditional complimentary close with a creative substitution. Rather than the empty "Sincerely," you replace tradition with a reminding message at the end like "PRINT POWERFULLY." This message then helps the customer remember how good you and your printing services are.

When customers remember you, you increase the chances they will do business with you. Bingo! That's what you want.

My last guarantee says you'll be able to use the ideas immediately. More than that, however, you'll also discover that writing is not nearly the chore it once was. Because you're using your creativity, you'll find that writing letters can be, of all things, fun.

The "how to" tips in the book make it easy for you to use the new ideas right away. So use them. Take the wraps off your old style and start on a new path. Then with your new style, you'll:

1. Save valuable time

2. Learn to be more creative

3. Accelerate your career

By reading *Business Letters That Get Results*, you'll discover trendsetting ideas that help you write quality business letters. Take advantage of what you learn. Give yourself a fresh, new look, and dress your business letters for results.

CHAPTER ONE

DRESS LETTERS FOR SUCCESS

Effective letter content is like an expensive suit. Both improve your odds for success.

It's indeed rare to receive a quality letter. When you do, you pay attention. This book, *Business Letters That Get Results*, will help you write quality letters that get noticed. In addition, you'll learn writing techniques that save time and make letter writing, of all things, fun.

This chapter sets the tone for the book's entire approach. And tone (the tone of your letters, that is) is exactly what this chapter covers.

What is tone? It's the ingredient that anticipates response, puts you in your reader's shoes, and lets you write what the reader wants to hear. It's like that distinguished look that John Molloy's *Dress For Success* suggests.

We've all heard of the successful principles in the book *Dress For Success*. In it we learned how managers and executives responded favorably to certain features of dress. Then, by following the suggestions, we had a better chance to succeed.

Why can't we apply the same success principles to business letters? We can and should. So let's dress business letters for success.

Effective letters work the same way Molloy's suggestions do. Both anticipate response to get results.

After receiving a business letter, we often ask, "What's in it for me?" If you ask that question, you better believe those who read your letters ask it, too. So your letters must have a solution that overcomes this questioning comment.

Effective tone lets you fashion that valuable writing solution. Rather than write about what's important to you (selling your product or service), you use a cooperative tone that tells customers what's important to them.

For instance, when you sell a recreational vehicle, you don't sell the vehicle. You sell what appeals to the customer—the exciting lifestyle, the comforts, and the fun. When selling a home, you don't sell a shelter. You sell what's important to the buyer—location, conveniences, and comfort. And when selling photography, you don't sell pictures. You sell what customers expect—remembrances.

In these examples, tone made the difference. It recognized the needs of others and put customers first.

We should take advantage of tone's appeal, too. With it we receive two distinct benefits:

1. Strengthened communication.

2. Saved time.

Tone's first benefit—strengthened communication
Our first benefit, strengthened communication, uses an element similar to the one *Dress For Success* uses: anticipation. Just as the clothes we wear affects others and how they respond to us, so do business letters. That means we must know what reaction to expect from our readers or customers. Normally we have three responses:

1. *A Positive or Receptive Response* (an outstanding appearance)
   These letters make others feel good. Here, you the writer say nice things like "thank you," "congratulations," or "I'll be there."

2. *A Neutral or Indifferent Response* (an adequate appearance)
   Sales or direct mail letters often fit into this category. Readers can often take or leave these letters. They couldn't care less. In fact, they just might toss these letters into the wastebasket.

3. *A Negative or Resistant Response* (cheap-fitting clothes)
   Ouch! These letters often complain or turn someone down. The language of no rears its ugly head with either a refusal or a denial.

Anticipating responses is not enough, however. You must also know how to improve them. In this book you'll learn how to improve responses. You'll learn how to

1. Strengthen the positive response.

2. Shift the neutral response to a positive response.

3. Shift the negative response to at least a neutral response.

Let's put these responses in language everyone understands. Strengthening a positive response is like making an "A" into an "A+" so you make someone feel really good. Shifting a neutral response to a positive response is like making a "C" into an "A" so customers read and act on your message. And changing the negative response to at least neutral is like improving an "F" to at least a "C" and, even better, to an "A," so customers favorably remember you.

Strengthening a positive response
First, let's explore how effective tone strengthens a positive response. It's especially powerful when you express thanks, give compliments, or agree to something. Instead of making someone feel just good, you make them feel terrific.

Here's an example in which you anticipate a positive response. Suppose a consultant, Fred, helped you solve a costly design problem for your assembly line. You want him to know how valuable he was to you.

Now what? Our first reaction would be "red flag." We've got to say *thanks*. So we write a *thank-you* letter, and it might start like this:

> Dear Fred:
>
> I want to take this opportunity to express my personal thanks for a job well done on the design work for the assembly-line design. We certainly appreciate the fine effort.

This kind of letter is one we all know should be written. We know Fred will appreciate the compliment. *But don't write that way.*

Why be satisfied with making others feel just good? Why take the easy way out and just write what's expected? Why write so you miss an opportunity to reinforce a positive feeling and make Fred and his firm feel truly special?

So what *do* you do? You take advantage of tone's strength and produce a letter that sparks a bond with Fred. This next letter takes advantage of tone's power. This letter not only reinforces the anticipated positive response, but it also encourages continued outstanding performance.

"YES" PLAN

> **YOU DID A TERRIFIC JOB, FRED:**
>
> Who would have believed the extent of the savings because of the design modification you made? I know I never expected results like that. Thanks for your wonderful help.
>
> When we hired you as a consultant we expected you to contribute to our profitability. You exceeded all expectations.
>
> The assembly-line design had been a serious headache for us. Success somehow seemed to elude us.
>
> That's when we called your firm in. You took over and gave us the design solution we were looking for. And in a short time, too.
>
> Fred, it was a treat working with you and your firm. Rest assured, when we need design help again, your company will be at the top of our list. Yes, I look forward to having you work with us again.

This example shows how effective tone works. Rather than just an ordinary note, effective tone helped us create an extraordinary letter.

Shifting the neutral response to a positive response
Next, let's examine the second response, indifference (or what we might call a neutral

response). Here we sell ourselves, our company, or our products and services. Then by anticipating an indifferent attitude, we use effective tone to develop a positive selling flavor. We dress our letters to anticipate what customers want, need, and demand.

Let's now explore tone's impact on others. Here are contrasting examples of a job application and a reply. The first examples don't anticipate. The second examples do.

Suppose a recent finance graduate, Andy Applicant, learns of a job opening at a bank. He wants the job. To be successful he must sell himself to the bank and explain why he is the one for the job. Unfortunately, he might come up with a weak letter like this:

```
I understand you have an opening in your bank for a recent
finance graduate. I'd like to be considered for that job.
Enclosed is my resume . . . .
```

Yawn, yawn, yawn. That letter sells nothing, contains no benefit for the bank, and certainly fails to hit an attention-getting hot button. It just starts with a fact and continues with self-serving comments. How boring. Unless the bank is desperate, the chances of a positive response are slim.

As a result of that indifference, the bank's Personnel Director may answer with this kind of letter:

```
Thank you for your letter applying for a job with us. We've
reviewed your resume and find it interesting. We will not,
however, be able to consider you now. We will keep your resume
on file for future reference. Good luck.
```

The bank's letter ignites no excitement and for good reason. The bank doesn't want to commit to an apparently weak applicant.

But effective tone creates a different mental picture. With it each party can change the dull letter into one that stands out, one that sells.

When applying for a job, we're selling ourselves. Expect a neutral response. So rather than deal from weakness (a negative response), Andy should use tone's strength to write a letter that sells his talents, creates a positive image, and says, "You'll make a smart decision by choosing me." Andy then could have written:

SALES PLAN

```
THINK PERFORMANCE! THINK ANDY APPLICANT, MS. BANKER

You want the job done and done well. You expect
dependability, reliability, and performance. You've
got it with ANDY APPLICANT. My resume (enclosed)
has all the details!

I GET THE JOB DONE
```

That letter opening rates as an attention getter. Here's someone who knows how to express himself and who makes first impressions count. His attention-getting letter gives the impression that he's a step above the crowd. He's letting his letter dress him for success.

The Personnel Director knows this applicant letter requires special handling and any answer is not enough. The bank wants to sell itself to Andy so they can talk to him. Consequently, the bank must project a good first impression. To achieve this, the Personnel Director uses effective tone to sell the bank and might then write:

YOU MAY BE THE ONE WE WANT, ANDY:

```
We're looking for an outstanding graduate to hire
in the bank. Your resume suggests you may be the
one to fill the job. Yes, we'd like to talk to you.
Call us at 555-5555.
```

_____ **IS A GREAT PLACE TO WORK!**

The difference in these examples is tone. By anticipating response and writing to fit that response, both Andy and the bank strengthened their worth with strong, persuasive letters. Yes, effective tone silenced indifference and turned the responses into positive ones.

Shifting the negative response to at least a neutral response
And last, tone gives us a third opportunity to turn around a negative feeling. This next situation arises with a customer complaint. Without effective tone helping answer the problem, we can lose the customer as well as the customer's positive word-of-mouth advertising. In fact, the customer may even begin to talk disparagingly about us to others. Who wants free advertising like that?

Many times when we answer a complaint, we try to correct it. The reason for this is easy. We want the customer to come back again.

Letters are often sent that seem to us to sound good. But do they really sound good to customers? Let's see with examples that show how tone strengthens response.

A charitable organization, XYZ Foundation, stayed at your hotel. After their stay, an invoice was sent to them. It included sales tax that should not have been charged. The Executive Director, Ms. Mary Meeting, has written and objected to the improper billing. Here's your response to her letter:

```
Dear Ms. Meeting:

Thank you for your May 4 letter. I'm sorry that our bookkeep-
ing department erroneously billed sales tax for your tax-ex-
empt organization. It never should have happened.

Accordingly, I am attaching a corrected bill, which I'm sure
you will find in order. If there is anything else we can do,
let us know.
```

Now let's examine that letter sentence by sentence. Is it all right? Does it use friendly language? Does it have a good tone? I don't think so. Here's why.

1. The first sentence thanked the customer for the complaining letter. Don't! Instead, tell the customer how smart she is to complain. Make her feel important.

2. The second sentence apologizes for the bookkeeping department's mistake. Oops! Since we're correcting the mistake, be positive and say what we're doing, not what we did. Further, by suggesting a particular department as the wrongdoer, we're suggesting that other departments may be equally prone to mistakes.

3. "It never should have happened." Of course not. But why even mention that it shouldn't have happened?

4. "Accordingly" sounds like stuffy lawyer talk. Avoid this language. Then that same sentence went on, ". . . you will find (the invoice) in order." The invoice better be in order. Otherwise, why send it?

5. "If there is anything else we can do, let us know." No sane person should ever use that language. These words say we'd be glad to fix another mistake. Customers don't want to hear about new problems; they want to solve the one at hand.

We've dissected that letter. Now, let's write a letter that uses tone to strengthen the message. Then we'd write like this:

SKIPPING APOLOGIES

YOU'RE RIGHT, MARY:

XYZ Foundation is tax exempt. The sales tax has been credited to your account. The corrected statement is being sent immediately.

Mary, you kept us on our toes when you were here. Now you're doing it again. Thanks. We look forward to working with you again.

Examine these comments about the second letter:

1. We immediately come to the point in the salutation and let Mary know she's right. We've made her feel important.

2. We then agree with her in the letter's first sentence and reinforce her attitude. Our message starts on a strong, positive note.

3. Next we tell her what action we've taken to correct her account. She never has to wonder what we're going to do. We've solved her complaint and made her feel good about herself, her complaint, and doing business with us.

4. Customers expect prompt response when they complain. Give it to them. "Immediately," let Mary know to expect prompt results.

5. The second paragraph started with Mary's first name, continued with a friendly approach that mentioned a familiar occurrence, and then said "thanks." These sentences should put Mary at ease and help us develop rapport.

6. By developing rapport, we've lowered Mary's resistance to us, and that lower

resistance makes it easier to do business with her again. So what do we do? We ask Mary to continue doing business with us in our last sentence.

The complaint answering examples showed us what to avoid, what to do, and how effective tone helps us. Then by using tone and anticipating Mary, we came up with a winning letter.

In our discussion of effective tone, we've seen how to make a good situation even better, how sales letters come alive, and how to turn around a complaint. We've seen how effective tone dresses your letters for success.

Tone's other benefit—saved writing time
In addition to stronger communication, effective tone gives us our second benefit—saved writing time.

When we want to impress others with how we dress, we have a list of tips to prevent stumbling and to help ensure added success. It's nothing more than a plan of action.

Using plans of action also prevents stumbling or struggling in our letters. In fact, writing struggles constantly emerge if we don't have a plan. And that struggle is easy to see in this next example.

A company's computer service warranty expired a month ago, and now it has major repair expenses. The company writes you to extend the warranty. Do you say no first? Is the letter personal? Is there language you should avoid?

In *Business Letters That Get Results*, you'll find a "No Plan" that helps you answer these questions. In addition, you'll also find other letter-strengthening plans like "Yes Plans," "Sales Plans," and "Complaint Plans."

Saving time when making someone feel good
Joan did excellent work on your research project. You've already told her how much her effort means to you and the company. But you want to do more. You want to write her a letter that strengthens your comments and further encourages her outstanding performance. How do you start? A typical letter might begin this way:

```
Dear Joan:

Thank you for your effort on the research project. It was a
job the company appreciates. We certainly recognize your valu-
able contribution.
```

That flattering letter is nice. It's a letter that leaves a wonderful impression. It gives an "A" response.

But why limit ourselves to just an "A"? Why not improve the letter so we get an "A+" response? We can.

How? Use my "Yes Plan." With it we have a blueprint for a time-saving outline that tells us how to truly reinforce a positive feeling. We'd then use these tips for our opening:

1. Praise the deed or person in the salutation.

2. Capitalize the salutation.

3. Include results or consequences in the first few sentences.

With these tips we'd have a letter that starts something like this:

"YES" PLAN

YOU WERE DYNAMITE, JOAN!!!

You gave us a valuable contribution that made a spectacular difference in the research project. It's easy to see why you're an important part of the research team.

FULL SPEED AHEAD!

The "Yes Plan" almost suggests the words we should use to make Joan feel terrific. Why? Because we focus our message and know our only priority is making Joan feel special. And the steps in the "Yes Plan" let us do that quickly.

Saving time when selling
Next, let's examine a sales letter. Let's see the suggestions that save us time.

With a sales letter we expect the classic "C" response. Our job is to turn an indifferent response into one that's positive. We want an "A." This next example shows how the "Sales Plan" helps.

Our restaurant, Fish Unlimited, has a banquet room available free for meetings. We want organizations, businesses, and special gatherings to use our facility and purchase our meals. How do we start a letter to get our targeted market to use our banquet room? How do we end it?

A typical letter might start this way:

Dear Decision Maker:

As General Manager of Fish Unlimited, I'd personally like to invite you to Fish Unlimited and offer you a very special opportunity. Our banquet room is now available for groups like yours. We'd like to have you and your people as customers.

That same letter may end like this:

If you have any questions, please call me at 111-1111. Thank you for this opportunity to introduce Fish Unlimited to you and your people.

Sincerely,

General Manager

On the surface those paragraphs seem fine. In fact, businesses use this kind of language all the time. And that's too bad. The language doesn't put the customer first in the beginning paragraph, and the last paragraph has the weak "please call me" for a call to action.

The General Manager wrote a letter that can obtain only limited results. Readers will probably throw the letter in the trash. For all practical purposes the letter is a waste of time.

To avoid the weak sales letter, I recommend the "Sales Plan," an effective outline approach that saves time. With it you have a timesaving outline that creates results. Here are a few of the steps:

1. Use a creative substitution to replace the salutation to grab attention.

2. Capitalize the creative substitution.

3. Use the first paragraph's beginning sentences to gain attention, create a need, and give a solution.

4. Use the first paragraph's last sentence to give a solution.

5. Use the last paragraph as a call to action. Use imperative sentences.

6. Use a capitalized creative substitution to replace the traditional complimentary close so you reinforce your message.

7. Use a P.S.

With those steps in mind, let's now write a new letter and see how it all comes together:

SALES PLAN

OUR BANQUET ROOM IS NOW AVAILABLE FREE!!!

Decision makers like you are always looking for quality meeting facilities. Even better, you'd like quality meeting facilities with tasty selections. You've got both at Fish Unlimited.

Let your people enjoy the relaxing comfort and tasty selections of Fish Unlimited. Tell yourself, "Yes, I want to look into what Fish Unlimited offers." Then call me at 111-1111. You'll be glad you made that call.

ENJOY THE HOSPITALITY OF FISH UNLIMITED,

General Manager

P.S. Remember to call early for your meeting or banquet reservations. <u>Call me today at 111-1111</u> for open dates.

The "Sales Plan" keeps us on target and gives us a plan of action for each part of the letter. In effect, the "Sales Plan" gives us a timesaving checklist that dresses sales letters for success.

Saving time when complaining

We've discussed the "Yes Plan" and the "Sales Plan." Let's examine another plan, the "Complaint Plan," and its timesaving results.

The Internal Revenue Service has, in our opinion, unjustly charged us $8,101. We treated equipment items as deductible expenses, and that caused a lower tax bill. The IRS says we should have depreciated them and, therefore, deductible expenses were excessive. As a result, the IRS is reducing our deductible expenses and increasing our taxes. We don't agree with this course.

With the typical complaint letters we use today, the letter might start like this:

```
Ladies and Gentlemen:

You're reducing our deductible expenses and increasing our
taxes. It's a procedure we don't understand.
```

I disagree with this approach. Letters like this are problem oriented, not solution oriented. As a result, they are just routine to anyone who handles them.

Rather than talk problems when complaining, I recommend a plan that aims at solutions, the "Complaint Plan." With this plan you take the guesswork out of complaints and never wonder what approach to follow. Here's an example of the "Complaint Plan" approach for handling the tax complaint:

COMPLAINT PLAN

```
CORPORATE CITIZENSHIP MEANS CORPORATE RESPONSIBILITY:

As corporate citizens we're always glad to pay our
taxes. But we don't owe any money and disagree with
your accounting approach. Credit us for $8,101.
```

Notice the difference. Rather than just state the problem, the second example asks for a solution and does it in a way that grabs attention.

That letter uses the first four steps of the "Complaint Plan."

1. Use a creative substitution as an attention getter.

2. Capitalize the creative substitution.

3. In the first few sentences of the first paragraph, reinforce the salutation.

4. In the last sentence of the first paragraph, ask for the solution you want.

Rather than use an empty salutation like "Ladies and Gentlemen," we replace it with a creative substitution, CORPORATE CITIZENSHIP MEANS CORPORATE RESPONSIBILITY. That replacement then immediately captures attention. After all, the IRS doesn't usually get letters like that.

Then rather than start the body of our letter with a problem, increased taxes, we use the first sentences to reinforce the creative substitution. These added attention-getting comments let the reader know something needs to be done.

The last sentence of the first paragraph asks for a solution, the $8,101 credit. The solution then creates an element of suspense, because the reader wants to know "why." This question, in turn, forces the reader to continue reading. The reader wants to know whether the solution is justified, what the problem actually is, and what needs to be done to solve the complaint.

The best part of that suspense is that you've planted a seed that suggests that your solution is the right one. With that seed planted, you increase your odds for success.

As you use the "Complaint Plan" to suggest solutions, you'll develop a discipline and pattern for every complaint. That discipline will translate into saved writing time.

The "Yes Plan," "Sales Plan," and "Complaint Plan" examples showed how the plans work. In these examples, we classified the letters and then used the appropriate plan. And by using the appropriate plan, we saved time, because we never had to start from scratch and reinvent the wheel.

SUMMARY
A well-dressed executive projects a quality image. A well-dressed letter also projects a quality image. The other chapters will discuss "how to" approaches that dress letters for that quality image. You'll learn writing techniques that will make you stand out.

CHAPTER TWO

THE SALUTATION AND COMPLIMENTARY CLOSE—DO WE NEED THEM?

Today's traditional salutations and complimentary closes are a tragedy. By sticking with these old-fashioned traditions, we're missing an opportunity to dress our letters for success.

If you could learn revolutionary letter writing techniques that would affect your career, your promotability, and your performance, would you be interested? Sure you would. We all would. And that's exactly what we're going to discuss.

We're going to break traditional letter-writing rules, challenge today's salutation and complimentary close, and replace them with a revolutionary approach, creative substitutions.

By using this approach, you'll learn fresh techniques that help your letters stand out, help them become more effective, and help take the struggle out of writing. In fact, you'll find that you'll not only be writing better letters, you'll have fun doing it.

Before we discuss creative substitutions, however, let's first examine today's tradition of the salutation and complimentary close.

We were first exposed to salutations and complimentary closes in school. Our teachers told us that we had to have a formal salutation and complimentary close in our letters. And it wasn't a question of whether we needed them, it was a question of where to put them. Then, after we learned where to put them, we learned what was expected of us in our letters. We had to have language like this:

Salutations	Complimentary Closes
Dear Ms. Smith	Sincerely
Dear Dr. Jones	Yours truly
Dear Friend	Best regards

Salutations	Complimentary Closes
To Whom It May Concern	Cordially
Dear Preferred Customer	Respectfully yours

Then we went into the business world and discovered we needed them there, too. And it didn't take long to justify why.

The boss tells us to write a letter. Since we're not fools, where do we go? We go to the files, of course, to see what the company has done before. What do we find? A letter the boss wrote. So what do we do? We do what the boss did. We use a salutation and complimentary close like the boss's.

Our daily lives confirm this tradition. Just look at your mail. We've all received letters that start "Dear Mr." or "Dear Ms." and end with "Sincerely" or "Yours truly."

And there is even more fuel for the tradition. Writing experts not only tell us to use the salutation and complimentary close, they tell what kind to use for different situations.[1]

Hogwash! How many times have you started your conversations, not letters, mind you, but conversations with "Ladies and Gentlemen" or "Dear Ms. Person"? How many times have you ended discussions and left a room waving goodbye and shouting "Yours truly" or "Sincerely"? If you started punctuating your talk with that kind of nonsense, friends and colleagues would probably consider you crazy.

But we use this language all the time when we write letters. After all, we're following a tradition that existed since before the turn of the century, even since Thomas Jefferson's day.

I say let's challenge the logic of the formal salutation and complimentary close. Let's discover a unique way to make letters stand out. Let's find a solution that discards the formal tradition and gives us a creative edge, a recipe for success.

Why? Because today's formal salutations and complimentary closes are a tragedy. They're stuffy, boring, and unimaginative. By sticking with this old-fashioned, horse-and-buggy tradition, we're missing an opportunity to strengthen our letters. Like yesterday's buggy whips, quill pens, and vacuum tubes, today's formal salutations and complimentary closes are outdated. They add nothing to results in today's marketplace.

Think about it. What do they add to today's business letter? Do they add color or personality? Do they capture attention? Do they add to the selling effort? Of course they don't. But they should.

My solution? Avoid the archaic tradition of formal salutations and complimentary closes. Replace them with creative substitutions, a powerful approach that lets you write the way you talk.

The creative substitution concept is revolutionary. And like Columbus, we're exploring a new world. We're going to find something new and exciting. We're going to find that the world of writing is not flat. We're going to find a new way.

Now let's explore what creative substitutions are. They're thoughts or messages that let us write salutations and complimentary closes the way we talk. This new approach replaces traditional salutations like "Dear Mr." or "Dear Ms." It replaces complimentary closes like "Sincerely" or "Yours truly." Rather than the humdrum of stuffy salutations and complimentary closes we're used to, we replace them with conversational language.

For instance, the thoughts or messages in salutations could be . . .

Thoughts	Messages
HELLO, MARY	WHAT A WONDERFUL IDEA, MR. SMITH
GOOD MORNING, FRED	THINK QUALITY. THINK _____
HI, TOMMY	MAKE IT HAPPEN AGAIN, GEORGE

Using these thoughts or messages is an easy way to eliminate "dear" in the salutation, which I have never understood.

REPLACING THE SALUTATION WITH A CREATIVE SUBSTITUTION

Why the creative substitution?
Here are three reasons for replacing the traditional salutation:

1. You expand initial attention and increase the odds your letters will be read and acted on.

2. You discover letter writing can actually be fun.

3. You open doors you never knew existed.

First, let's examine why we improve our results with the creative substitution. The first five seconds in a sales letter often determine whether a reader or customer will continue. So we know that the initial attention is critical in any letter we write. What do we do? We carefully craft a powerful, attention-getting first paragraph to capture those first five seconds.

With creative substitutions, we expand the initial attention-getting five seconds. Rather than limiting ourselves to our initial paragraph, we inject an attention-getting message before the thoughts of the first paragraph. In effect, we expand the customer's attention span.

Then by expanding those five seconds, we increase the odds our letters will be read, remembered, and acted on. Isn't that why we write a letter in the first place?

Second, you'll find that writing letters can actually be fun. Instead of being tied to tradition, you'll tap your creative juices and discover a whole new way to write. One person, Marianne Dunn of Dunn & Associates, heard me talk on creative substitutions and now uses my approach. She wrote this:

THANK YOU

```
YOU'VE DONE THE IMPOSSIBLE, JAY!

You have made letter writing fun! For as long as I
can remember I have hated to write letters—boring!
I don't think I'll ever approach the task in quite
the same way. Thanks!
Marianne Dunn
Dunn & Associates
```

Others who have heard me talk on creative substitutions and who also use this approach tell me the same story. They *will not* go back to the old way. They tell me that creative substitutions are too much fun. Besides, they get results. For instance, one client,

Warren Gale of Positive Reflections, wrote:

```
"It's fun writing exciting letters. It's even more fun getting
exciting results."
```

Finally, here's another reason to use creative substitutions. They'll help you open writing doors you never knew existed. You'll discover approaches that make you stand out with customers, peers, and friends. You'll have a tool that creates goodwill, makes others feel special, and turns ordinary letters into valuable sales letters.

Now let's support that thought. A few months ago, a friend who used my approach, Jim Swann of IBM, introduced me to a Rotary audience. Then he added this: "You're going to hear some new ideas. They work. In fact, expect to get more mail if you use these ideas. I started using Jay's ideas at the office for my electronic mail. The responses to my messages increased about 50%."

Capitalizing the creative substitution

Whenever you use a creative substitution, capitalize every letter in it. You do so for one reason—attention.

When you read a newspaper or magazine, do you read the copy or the headlines first? You read the headlines. These publications use the visual technique of the headline to make their messages stand out. Of course, they have the advantage of being able to use larger type; you need to find something comparable. Like the pros, take advantage of the visual effect of the headline. Capitalize your creative substitution.

```
DON'T USE: What a terrific letter, Carol!

USE: WHAT A TERRIFIC LETTER, CAROL!
```

By capitalizing the creative substitution, you're compounding the attention the reader gives to your message. First, the creative substitution attracts attention, since most letters do not use this approach. Second, you're using a visual technique that attracts the eye and creates curiosity in the reader.

Let's go one step further. Many word processors and computers have the capability of creating bold lettering. If you have that capability, use it for the creative substitution. By using bold lettering, you're dressing your letter for success.

Purposes for using creative substitution

You use a creative substitution whenever you want to create friendliness, attention, or both. Like the physical law that states, "A body in motion tends to stay in motion," a creative substitution helps customers, colleagues, and friends continue their reading momentum.

Creating added friendliness

Friendliness always exists when you write to someone you know. So when you write a friend or colleague, use that person's first name coupled with a creative substitution. You'll intensify the friendliness of your message. For instance,

- **YOU REALLY ARE SPECIAL, FRANK**

- **WHAT A SUPER JOB, LANCE**

- **YOU DID IT AGAIN, BETTY**

- **YOU MADE MY DAY, PAUL**

- **WE COULDN'T HAVE DONE IT WITHOUT YOU, SARA**

Who wouldn't want to continue reading a letter that starts with flattering creative substitutions like these? The impact will hook anyone.

Capturing added attention

A second purpose for using the creative substitution arises when you want attention. A sales letter fits here because you *always* want an attention grabber in a sales letter. Picture how this next example grabs attention:

WHY <u>PERFORMANCE UNLIMITED</u> FOR YOUR TRAINING, MS. ARMSTRONG?

If you received a letter with a creative substitution that asked a question, one thing would happen. You'd want to read on. The mind almost insists that we try to answer questions. Now extend that same thought process to your readers and customers. They'll want to read on, too.

Here's another example, but without a question:

JUST PICK UP THE PHONE, MR. JONES

Readers will want to continue with a creative substitution like this. That thought is not a question, but readers will still feel compelled to read on as if it were a question. They still want to know *why* they should pick up the phone.

Coupling friendliness with attention

No matter what your purpose, if you use a creative substitution, you always couple friendliness with attention. They go hand in glove. So let's further probe the power of the creative substitution.

A compliment probably shows the creative substitution's power better than anything else. Imagine how you would respond if someone wrote you a flattering letter that starts with this salutation:

YOU DID A TERRIFIC JOB, (your first name)

You'd not only read the entire letter, but you'd probably take it home and show it to your spouse! Expect others to respond the same way.

Now let's compliment someone else. Suppose Barbara, a hotel sales manager you worked with, made a significant impact on the success of your recent convention. You want to let her know how special she is. If you followed tradition, you'd start your letter "Dear Barbara." And she'd like the favorable comments that would follow.

But why be satisfied with the ordinary, with tradition? Why not let her know how truly special she is? Why not craft a letter that jumps at her and shouts "You are special"? You can do that with a creative substitution like this:

WHAT A DIFFERENCE YOU MADE, BARBARA

Put another way, you've written a keeper. You can expect three responses. One, she'll hang on to it (most of us never receive letters written that way). Two, she may call you and give you her special thanks (we all like to share good news). Three, she'll remember you and how good you are. Translation—you produced powerful goodwill.

Now why would I say you can expect three responses? Easy. People have responded in exactly these ways when they have received letters like this from me. And others who follow this pattern also attest to these kinds of results.

Attention grabs the reader

A sales letter always needs to start with an attention grabber. So think of the creative substitution as the equipment needed to start any sales letter. You never think of playing baseball without a bat. Likewise, never think of starting any sales letter without a creative substitution. It adds necessary attention that gets your message off and running.

Look at these next examples. Each will grab your attention. And notice that each adds suspense with "it."

- **IT'S REVOLUTIONARY**
- **YOU CAN DO IT**
- **MAKE IT HAPPEN**

"It," however, is not your only weapon. Other approaches also work. Check out these examples. They'll get your attention, too.

- **TAKE ADVANTAGE OF US**
- **MAKE A DIFFERENCE**
- **WHEN YOU THINK COMPUTERS, THINK _____**

Maybe you have a complaint. Then you want satisfaction. For that satisfaction, you must get attention immediately and let the reader know a problem exists. The creative substitution gives you that attention. And with the reader's attention, you increase the probability of the answer you want.

Here are examples you might use; each suggests that a problem exists:

- **FROSTY THE SNOWMAN WOULD MELT**
- **I NEED YOUR HELP**
- **IT DOESN'T ADD UP**

Group recognition

Are you part of the masses? Do you want to be identified as one of the masses? Do you prefer impersonal language like "Dear Occupant" or "Dear Home Owner"?

No! All of us want to be recognized as individuals. Yet in much of today's mail, we consistently see language like "Dear Chamber of Commerce Member," "Dear Employee," "Dear Credit Card Holder." Those general statements at the start of a letter are nothing more than tradition. And because they follow tradition, they're convenient.

Because they are convenient, many feel traditional identification in letters is necessary when writing to groups. In fact, we're often told we need to acknowledge the group we're writing to[2]. The theory goes that traditional identification creates a bond of familiarity between the seller and the customer. So salutations like these are used:

- DEAR INVESTORS

- DEAR SUBSCRIBER

- MY FELLOW REAL ESTATE FRIENDS

- DEAR GOLFERS

- DEAR AUTOMOBILE DEALERS

I disapprove of these salutations. I think we should avoid identifying people as part of the masses or a large group. And I'm not alone. At one of my workshops, a member of the audience volunteered this information. She told me that her bank had used this approach with depositors. Her bank letter started, "Dear Valued Customer."

"Hold on," she said. "If I'm so valued, why didn't the bank use my name?"

So she went to the bank and complained. And she wasn't the only one. She learned that others had the same objection.

That bank story tells me we can do a better job. We should break with the past, be different, and come up with something original. Here's how. Rather than the traditional "Dear Friend," build a letter that starts with an attention-getting comment, the creative substitution that substitutes for the traditional salutation.

Then, by using the creative substitution, fashion a message that works like the first sentence in the letter. Think about it. If the letter's first sentence attracts attention, why not use it as a headline before the letter? You can only make your letter stronger. Here are examples of what we might have done in the past and what we should do in the future:

For a health item
> WRONG: Dear Health Enthusiast
>
> RIGHT: **IT MAKES A DIFFERENCE**

A sales message
> WRONG: Dear Customer
>
> RIGHT: **GET ON THE BANDWAGON**

For a new store
> WRONG: Dear Friend
>
> RIGHT: **LET'S GET TOGETHER**

For an association meeting
```
WRONG: Dear Association Member
```

```
RIGHT: YOU MAKE THE DIFFERENCE! BE THERE!
```

For a questionnaire
```
WRONG: Dear Colleague
```

```
RIGHT: TELL IT LIKE IT IS
```


Informality
While we've talked about using thoughts or messages as a creative substitution for the traditional salutation, we do have an informal situation that needs comment. With a handwritten note you already have something that screams attention, the note itself. The personal, handwritten note announces to others how special the reader is.

Added attention may not be necessary. So just write the first name as acknowledgment. It's all you need. This gets rid of "Dear."

REPLACING COMPLIMENTARY CLOSES WITH CREATIVE SUBSTITUTIONS
The traditional complimentary close uses language like "Yours truly" or "Sincerely." We're all familiar with it. All we have to do is look at our daily correspondence. This language exists in almost everything we receive.

To reinforce using the language of "Yours truly" or "Sincerely," look at grammar books. Most are alike and suggest that "Yours truly" is more formal than "Sincerely."[3] Who cares? That language is crazy. All it does is give an empty statement.

Examine the traditional complimentary close. Does it create friendliness? Does it persuade? Does it help others remember? No!

Generally, the complimentary closes you see in business letters *are* traditional. Trite would be another way to describe them. Use them if you want a 90-pound weakling to send your message.

Rather than weakness, however, I suggest that you use strength. And that strength comes with using a creative substitution that replaces the traditional complimentary close. With it you deviate from what you normally see, challenge an outdated tradition, and inject a positive tone with either a thought or message.

This approach might then say "HAVE A TERRIFIC YEAR" or "COME ON IN" rather than "Best wishes" or "Respectfully yours." In effect, the change lets you spice up the end of your letter.

Let's investigate why you replace the traditional complimentary close with a creative substitution. There are three reasons:

1. Helping others remember.

2. Creating friendliness.

3. Grabbing attention.

With the first reason you help readers and customers remember your message. Let's say you go to a football game and six touchdowns are scored; the last one in the final thirty seconds wins the ballgame. Which touchdown do you remember? The last. And where is the complimentary close? Last.

Creative substitution creates that same kind of remembering. By being last, the creative substitution leaves a thought or idea with the reader. As the last thought, it reminds readers or customers of the entire letter they just read. Do "Sincerely" and "Yours truly" remind them of the letter content?

Here are examples that recapture a letter's earlier comments and show the reminding effect:

- **TAKE ADVANTAGE OF THE BENEFITS**

- **IT WILL HELP YOU WITH LONG-TERM SURVIVAL**

- **IMAGINE ITS MONEY SAVING EFFECT**

A second reason is friendliness. By being friendly, you're presenting a special warmth. Using a friendly substitution is like putting a smile on your letter. If you received a letter that ended on a cheery note, you'd probably be cheery, too. A smile is contagious!

So if a friendly end to a letter captures your interest, it will capture interest in your readers, too. Here are examples:

- **HAVE A PROFITABLE DAY**

- **SEE YOU FOR LUNCH**

- **CONGRATULATIONS AGAIN**

- **HAVE A GREAT 1992**

- **ENJOY YOUR TRIP TO NEW YORK**

Finally, you use the creative substitution for attention. Let's explore how the creative substitution generates attention by being different.

Newspapers write articles about automobile accidents. TV programs cover interesting items like political flip-flops. And magazines tell us about the rich and the famous. The reasoning is easy to understand. Because the stories are out of the ordinary, they're different. And because they are extraordinary, they catch our attention.

Creative substitution works the same way. Because it's different, it attracts attention. "Sincerely" and "Yours truly" don't. Those traditional closes do nothing.

In a persuasive letter, however, you want your complimentary close to help create a solution, to get results. So do something to help customers remember how good you and your product are. Be different. Use a creative substitution. Notice how these next examples, ones you could easily adopt for your own use, capture attention:

- **INVEST IN YOURSELF**

- **IMAGINE HOW IT CAN HELP YOUR CAREER**

- **JOIN THE FUN**

- **LET'S PUT SOMETHING TOGETHER FOR YOUR TEAM**

- **ENJOY THE HOSPITALITY OF _____**

Remember the three reasons we challenge traditional complimentary closes: to help others remember, to create friendliness, and to grab attention. Then take advantage of how the creative substitution works. You'll be glad you did.

Now let me give you added examples to help you get started on this approach:

- **INVEST IN YOUR FAMILY** (an insurance company)
- **PRINT POWERFULLY** (a printer)
- **SELL PROFITABLY** (a sales consulting firm)
- **QUALITY AT A HIRE LEVEL** (a headhunting firm)
- **LET US DO THE PLANNING** (a convention hotel)

PUNCTUATING CREATIVE SUBSTITUTIONS

Traditional punctuation says to put a colon (:) after the salutation and a comma (,) after the complimentary close. I also recommend this punctuation with creative substitutions. But I recommend more, too.

You don't have to limit yourself to the colon after the salutation. One approach replaces it with an ellipsis (. . .). Then the letter starts:

LOOK AT IT, MS. SMITH . . .

In some instances, you may want the creative substitution to extend beyond the salutation. You want it to be the beginning of a sentence continued in the body of the letter. Then use ellipses at both the end of the creative substitution and at the beginning of the body of the letter. Here's an example:

IT WAS NICE MEETING YOU, MARY . . .

. . . at the Chamber committee meeting last Friday.

Since we often start letters with questions, why not put them in the salutation, too? Then you need a question mark. Here's what we'd have then:

WHAT'S A COMPETITIVE ADVANTAGE, MR. THOMPSON?

Everyone wants it. But how do you get it? We can help . . . .

For letters that compliment, I suggest one to three exclamation points after the creative substitution. Then the creative substitution is like this:

YOU WERE SPECTACULAR, TOM!!!

The exclamation points add pizzazz to the nice remark you have already made. In effect, you are getting extra bang for your message.

Now let's look at the complimentary close. The comma always works. But, again, let's not limit ourselves to that alone.

Rather than the traditional comma, you can substitute an ellipsis. Since the creative substitution for the complimentary close is unconventional, you'll often want to be unconventional here, too. The ellipsis lets you do that. The letter then ends:

```
ENJOY THE FUN . . . .
```

The last kind of punctuation for the complimentary close is the exclamation point. Use one to three here also. Then you would see:

```
ENJOY THE FUN!!!
```

Be careful with exclamation points. Professional writers try to stay away from the exclamation point. They feel it is overworked and often gives a false sense of emphasis. It can detract from writing. I agree.

For instance, in a sales letter, you should never use them in the salutation. You're creating a false sense of urgency. Being different is enough. Why add false emphasis?

And in any letter, you should never use them for both the salutation and the complimentary close. Don't clutter your letters with them. Do use them if you think they fit. But only once.

DO CREATIVE SUBSTITUTIONS WORK?

They sure do; let's see how by examining results and including comments other have made about this approach.

Results

Here are two examples that show results from using creative substitutions:

1. A professional speaker from Dallas was trying to speak before the National Association of Realtors at their national convention. She had read an article of mine about creative substitutions and immediately changed her approach. Here's the way she started her letter to the Association:

   ```
   GOOD GRIEF, CAROL . . .

   What's happening to real estate?
   ```

   She presented two programs totaling four and a half hours for that Association. She got the job on her merits. The letter got her the attention she needed to show her merits.

2. A local printing company asked me to prepare a direct mail piece for them. Their letter had a salutation that started, "TAKE ADVANTAGE OF US." The complimentary close said, "PRINT POWERFULLY." When I asked about the results, I heard this, "We only got 80 replies."

   Then I asked how many letters were sent out. The answer—600. That's a 13.3% response—beyond any reasonable expectation for a direct mail piece.

What others say

Others also support this revolutionary approach. Here's what they say:

```
You've revolutionized my writing, Jay. The creative substitu-
```

tions are a writing breakthrough. My life will never be the same because of what I learned from you.

Madeline Kline
M.I. Kline, Inc.
Scarsdale, NY

• • •

Your approach has revolutionized my letters . . . The acceptance from my clients and friends has generated many compliments. I enjoy that.

Eugene Frazier
Eugene Frazier Studio, Inc.
Dallas, TX

• • •

Your ideas about creative substitutions are dynamite.

Dick Richard
Vice-President, Director of Marketing
Sun Country Destinations
Scottsdale, AZ

• • •

You opened new doors and helped me distinguish myself in the business world. Gone forever are "Dear Jay's," "Sincerely yours," and ho-hum writing. Now my letters have punch.

Maureen G. Mulvaney
President, MGM & Associates
Phoenix, AZ

• • •

Your ideas stimulate an aggressive approach, while at the same time personalizing as if you were talking one on one.

Deborah Loyd
Vice President of Programs
North Texas Hotel Sales and Marketing Association
Arlington, TX

BENEFITS OF CREATIVE SUBSTITUTION

So far you've read about a new approach to writing, creative substitutions. Now let's discuss the specific benefits you receive by using them.

For you
Expect three benefits when you use creative substitutions.

1. You focus your message.

2. Others respond in kind.

3. Letter writing doesn't have to be a struggle.

The most important reason to use creative substitutions is that you focus your message. You immediately come to the point and know what you are going to write about. Here's how this focusing helped me.

I put on a writing seminar for the United Way of Tarrant County and its participating agencies over two years ago. Ariel Hunter was the meeting planner and had been a tremendous help for me. So I wrote her a letter of thanks after the seminar.

Using the traditional salutation, I probably would have started something like this:

```
Dear Ariel:

Thank you very much for the help you gave me at the seminar.
That help made my work a lot easier . . . .
```

She would have liked that letter since we all like letters of thanks. They tell us we did a good job.

But I wasn't satisfied with the traditional way to write her a letter of thanks. Rather than put the emphasis on thanks, I wrote her a letter that put her first and focused on what she had done. Here's what I wrote:

"YES" PLAN

```
YOUR PROFESSIONALISM SHOWED, ARIEL:

When you said that you would handle the
preliminaries for the seminar, I was impressed.
When you provided name plates for the participants,
I was impressed. And when you made a suggestion
during the seminar on how to improve it, I was
impressed. You're a pro. Thanks for your help.

Ariel, it was a treat working with you. Yes, you
made my job easy. Without question, I look forward
to working with you again.

WRITE POWERFULLY,
```

This letter focused on Ariel and what she had done. And the impact went beyond what I had expected.

Not long ago at a professional meeting, I ran into Ariel, whom I hadn't seen for over two years. She saw me first and made it a point to come over and talk to me. She said she was no longer with the United Way and was working elsewhere.

Then she added this thought, "Jay, I still have your letter. I use it now to remind me how to write thanks to others. It's been a great help." For Ariel the focus of that letter had been quite powerful. You'll also find that creative substitutions focus your message and give letters added strength.

The second benefit for you is that others will respond in kind. When you write with this style, you've helped others challenge their traditional thinking, and encouraged them to write with creative substitutions, too. Let me explain.

Recently, I spoke to the Sales and Marketing Executives of Fort Worth. To coordinate the handouts, I had to write Vi Baker, the organization's Executive Director. My letter to her ended with this complimentary close, "EXPECT A FUN PROGRAM"

She answered with a confirming letter on the program's details. She started her letter with a salutation that said, "I KNOW WE'LL HAVE A FUN PROGRAM."

By using that language, she had echoed what I had written. And by adopting that style, we had developed a special bond even though we had not yet met. You can expect similar results.

With the third benefit of creative substitution, you'll discover that letters are not the struggle they've been in the past.

Here's what Wayne Pickering of the Health Aquarium in Daytona Beach wrote about using creative substitutions: "I knew I had a day of correspondence ahead of me. Your ideas helped take the drudgery out of writing and I'm grateful! THANKS!"

His comment is easy to understand. He was armed with a fresh approach to letter writing. Rather than being tied to tradition, he had an opportunity to use his creative juices so he could actually have fun writing his correspondence. For instance, his salutation in his letter to me read:

```
THANKS A MILLION, JAY!
```

Imagine how he must have felt throwing out the old and replacing it with words he *wanted* to say. You too can experience that same feeling. Just throw out the old and replace it with a creative substitution.

For your customer
Creative substitutions affect customers and help them remember your benefits—and what those benefits can do for them. Let me explain.

When we get orders from new customers, we know we have to thank them. We're conditioned to think "red flag." We need to write them. Often letters like this are written:

```
Dear Donna:

Thank you very much for your new order. We certainly appreciate
it and will do everything to maintain your confidence in us.
```

You can do better than that. Use the creative substitution to create impact. Let customers know how smart they are for picking your product and start your letter like this:

THANK YOU

```
YOU'LL LIKE YOUR DECISION, DONNA:
```

```
With your selection of _____, you'll notice an
immediate improvement in quality. There are
numerous benefits in store for you, including
_____, _____, and _____. We sure
look forward to working with you!
```
YOU MADE THE RIGHT CHOICE

With a letter like this, the customer will definitely remember you and your products. You have, in effect, strengthened the customer's initial decision. And with this approach, you certainly should have no problem with buyer's remorse.

Let's continue this discussion on impact. Suppose you work for a hotel and have been trying to get an association to have its annual convention at your facility. The association picked another hotel in your city.

In this situation don't think of the association's selection as a rejection. Think of it as an opportunity for future business. Creative substitutions help you do this. Then you'd write this kind of letter:

THANK YOU

YOU'LL LIKE YOUR DECISION, FRED:
```
The ABC Hotel is a quality hotel. I'm confident
you'll enjoy the facility. For future conventions,
however, come to our hotel. We feel the quality of
_____ is even better.
```
ENJOY YOUR STAY IN DALLAS . . . .

How many association meeting planners *ever* receive a letter like this? If they did, they'd remember your courteous approach. And that's what you want them to do—remember.

So whenever you've been told no, think of how your product might benefit the prospect in the future. Then write a letter that compliments the competition and, at the same time, suggests you are even better. That letter creates impact and will pay future dividends.

For your company
Your improved communication skills will make you more valuable to the company.

By using creative substitutions you know that letter writing is not nearly the chore it had been. That means you'll have to spend less time to get out quality letters. Less time in turn frees you for other productive work.

In effect, you discover you are in a win-win situation. The company gains because of your talents. Your talents help you gain by developing your visibility and promotability.

Hope Anderson of San Diego Gas & Electric wrote this to me after adopting my ideas: "GIVE YOURSELF A PAT ON THE BACK, JAY . . . . You've helped me develop a reputation as an 'ace' letter writer."

Then about a year later she wrote and told me she had gotten a promotion. Yes, her new writing skills had contributed worth both to her and to her company!

DROPPING SALUTATIONS AND COMPLIMENTARY CLOSES

Do you ever drop a salutation and complimentary close? Yes, in some circumstances. With this approach, you benefit three ways:

1. By eliminating the salutation's empty identification.

2. By making selected correspondence impersonal.

3. By eliminating wasted effort.

Now let's explore these benefits.

We might find ourselves in trouble with an organization like the Internal Revenue Service. We have no idea of the identity of the person who will receive our letter.

So what do we do? We could follow tradition and use salutations like "Gentlemen" or "Dear Sir." But these salutations only start a letter with empty language that identifies no one. Besides, the "Dear Sir" or "Gentlemen" letter may go to a woman.

And if people wanted to eliminate sexism, they'd say something like "Ladies and Gentlemen." Those words, however, sound like language from the circus. But guess what? There are authorities[4] who suggest this is the correct approach!

I challenge those authorities. It's empty language. Rather than use it, drop it. Any time you're writing an unknown party, *drop the salutation* and go directly from the inside address to the body of the letter. Why write that intangible and evasive "Ladies and Gentlemen" or other similar language?

For instance, drop the salutation in a routine letter that requests information from an association you've had no prior contact with. Drop it if you're writing for information advertised in a magazine. And drop it when requesting something from a company and you're writing a department.

When you don't have a name and write a department like Financial or Public Relations, just mention the department in the inside address. Then after writing the inside address, go right to the body of the letter. Follow this example:

```
Public Relations Department
XYZ Corporation
One Main Street
Anywhere, TX
Please send me . . . .
```

The second benefit seems a little odd—you make your letters impersonal. But consider a letter in which you are writing a negative message like turning someone down for a job. In those letters you always want to be impersonal.

When writing no, never say "Dear" anybody. That language is inconsistent with what you're writing. In addition, the traditional complimentary closes like "Yours truly" and "Sincerely" add formality to your message. Writing no is hard enough. Why inject further stilted style with a formal complimentary close?

There is an exception to the no letter's complimentary close. In a few no letters you may discover you want to use a friendly complimentary close. For instance, in a job denial you may have become friendly with the job applicant. You could want a personal complimentary close like GOOD LUCK. Whatever you do, though, omit the salutation.

Now let's examine the complaint letter. As mentioned earlier in this chapter, use a creative substitution in the salutation to create attention (I NEED YOUR HELP). But always drop the complimentary close to be impersonal. Just sign your name at the end of the letter.

For example, suppose some company cheated you out of $735.21. Signing "Sincerely" is like saying, "I'm mad as heck, love and kisses." Rather, go directly from the body of the letter to the signature. Be all business. Eliminate any suggestion of friendliness. Drop the complimentary close.

Next, to eliminate wasted effort, it sometimes makes sense to drop the salutation and complimentary close. If the traditional salutation is empty, you add language that you shouldn't have to type. By eliminating the salutation and complimentary close you're saving the time and effort of typing those words. Over a year, that could mean a number of typed lines.

Large and small corporations have policies that eliminate the salutation and complimentary close in all *internal* correspondence. Why? To save time and money.

Since their only purpose with internal correspondence is to communicate, why add the fluff of salutations and complimentary closes? They just add costs for dictation, typing, and reading. And costs only increase the expense of doing business. So saving time and money becomes a wonderful motivator.

So what do they do? Here are three examples:

```
To:
From:
Subject:
```

• • •

```
Mr. Mike Motivator
Fifth Floor
```

• • •

```
Ms. Connie Convincer
New York, NY
```

In each of these examples the complete inside address disappears and is replaced with a direct, time-saving approach.

SUMMARY

Change the way you write letters; drop traditional salutations and complimentary closes, then replace them with creative substitutions. This new style of writing will help you and your writing stand out with customers, clients, and friends. In effect, you give yourself a competitive advantage with an attention-getting difference.

    1. Replace salutations with creative substitutions.

        a. Why you use the creative substitution.

            • It expands initial attention and increases the odds letters will be read and acted on.

- It makes letter writing fun.
- It opens new doors.

   b. Always capitalize creative substitutions.

   c. Reasons for using the creative substitution.

- It creates added friendliness.
- It captures attention.
- It couples friendliness with attention.
- It improves group recognition.

2. Replace complimentary closes with creative substitutions.

   a. Reasons for using the creative substitution.

- It helps others remember.
- It creates friendliness.
- It grabs attention.

   b. Always capitalize creative substitutions.

3. Punctuation for creative substitutions.

   a. Traditional punctuation: the colon and comma.

   b. Ellipses.

   c. Question marks.

   d. Exclamation points.

4. Benefits of creative substitutions.

   a. For you.

- To focus messages.
- To help others respond in kind.
- To help eliminate letter writing struggles.

   b. For customers.

- To help them remember what you can do for them.

   c. For your company.

- To make you a more valuable employee.

5. Reasons to drop salutations and complimentary closes.

   a. To eliminate the salutation's empty identification.

   b. To make certain correspondence impersonal.

   c. To eliminate wasted effort.

CHAPTER THREE

SKIPPING APOLOGIES

This innovative approach to writing strong, positive business letters means never having to say "I'm sorry."

"Man cannot live by words alone, despite the fact that sometimes he has to eat them."

— Adlai Stevenson

We never want to eat our words. In business letters we especially don't want to eat crow, because letters can be unforgivingly permanent. So it's important that we get a positive flavor in our letters.

Here's an easy technique to make your correspondence more positive. Quit using the words "I'm sorry" in any letter. Whenever you're tempted to say "I'm sorry" in a letter, don't.

"Wait a minute," you're probably saying. "Others expect us to apologize when something bad happens."

You're right—if you are the wrongdoer in an accident or mistake. As the wrongdoer, it makes sense to apologize, to say I'm sorry. The injured party expects an in-person apology. Besides, an apology can make you feel better and reduce stress.

In a letter, though, "I'm sorry" never makes sense. You've distanced yourself from the situation and now want to present a favorable image. Here are three reasons "I'm sorry" should never appear in any business letter:

1. "I'm sorry" has a negative tone.

2. "I'm sorry" reminds others of bad situations or disappointments.

3. We shouldn't apologize for something we had no control over.

AVOIDING A NEGATIVE TONE

First, let's examine the negative tone of "I'm sorry." Just look at those words. Do they suggest something good has happened, a positive result, a favorable situation? Of course not.

The following conversations show how we avoid that negative language. Notice in these next examples how you strengthen conversations with positive comments like "I wish" or "I wanted" rather than using the negative "I'm sorry."

Suppose Fred, a stockbroker, sees you received a poor fill on an execution to buy a stock. Fred injects negative tone into his language when he says, "I'm sorry you didn't get a better fill." That language immediately puts Fred on the defensive. He would improve his conversation with a positive word selection like, "I wish you had gotten a better fill."

Or suppose someone telephoned you while you were away from your desk. You call back and say, "I'm sorry I wasn't at my desk when you called." You make that statement positive by saying, "I wanted to be here when you called." That way you make others feel important by putting them first.

With mistakes, customers want positive results. Write about those positive results. Let customers know that you are either correcting the situation, taking steps to ensure the situation doesn't happen again, or both. These next examples show the dramatic contract between the negative "I'm sorry" and corrective or positive action:

```
WRONG: I'm sorry an error in your account occurred.
RIGHT: Your account has been corrected.

WRONG: I'm sorry the mistake occurred.
RIGHT: Your suggestion was right on the money.

WRONG: I'm sorry the procedure caused you a delay.
RIGHT: You're right. We should have given you better help to
       get to the airport. The situation you mentioned has been
       corrected. Thanks for bringing it to our attention.

       And to show you our appreciation for your past busi-
       ness, the next time you use our hotel anywhere in the
       country, the room is on us.
```

Sally Shopper orders a product from us that we don't make. Even though we are unable to fill the order, our thinking tells us we still want to help. We want to imagine her as a potential customer, as someone who may eventually do business with us, or as someone who might refer a customer.

We nip that thinking in the bud by using the negative "I'm sorry." Those words assure us of getting off on the wrong foot. This reply letter shows why:

```
I'm sorry we will be unable to fill your order. We do not make
that kind of product. We do make the widget, though. We've
enclosed a circular on it.
```

1. The first sentence starts by apologizing for something we can't do. It almost shouts, "We can't help you." Imagine how the potential customer feels with "I'm sorry" as the first words in the letter. Goodwill is the last thought that comes to

mind.

2. The second sentence continues the negative tone and says what we can't do, not what we can do.

3. The third sentence is a joke. The first two sentences created a negative tone. Now the reader is asked to look at our product. Don't count on that.

4. The last sentence is a continuation of the previous sentence. Since the reader wasn't helped, why should the brochure ever be opened?

Now we change the letter. Our purpose is to make the other person, Sally Shopper, feel glad about contacting us. We know that she may talk to others about the friendly way we handle business, may refer someone else to us, or may become a potential customer for our products.

So what do we do? We give Sally a solution to her immediate problem. So without the negative "I'm sorry," we might then write:

SKIPPING APOLOGIES

```
I wish we could fill your order. Our firm makes
widgets rather than the item you ordered. We can
help, though. XYZ Corporation manufactures that
product. You can contact them at:

XYZ Corporation
100 Main Street
Anywhere, CA 11111

GOOD LUCK WITH FILLING YOUR ORDER

P.S. Whenever you are in the market for a widget,
give us a holler. We'll be glad to help. A brochure
on our widget is enclosed.
```

Here are the positive ideas the first paragraph uses:

1. Rather than apologizing for not making a product, the letter starts with a positive message that says "we'd like to help." Reader response has to be favorable.

2. The second sentence says what we make, not what we don't make.

3. Next, we give a solution and say who can help. Isn't that refreshing to read?

4. Then we give the specifics of how to contact a company who makes the product. That's extending a helping hand and showing that our company cares about others.

The second paragraph is just one sentence and extends the idea of hope. That thought is a nice way to end a letter.

The P.S. takes advantage of an opportunity created by goodwill. If the potential customer ever needs our product, we've planted a seed that says we are the one.

Notice that the first paragraph and P.S. both use the word "help." By skipping apologies and stressing help, we've left the potential customer with the idea that we are a *helping* company, that we'd be a good company to work with. Think of the goodwill this message creates. And it costs only a postage stamp. "I'm sorry" undermines a positive approach. "I wish" puts others first. And whenever we put someone else first, that's effective communication.

AVOIDING THE REMINDER OF BAD SITUATIONS OR DISAPPOINTMENTS

Here's the second reason to avoid "I'm sorry." *It reminds others of bad situations or dissatisfaction.* Since you can't control the past, why even bring it up? These words just remind us of a problem or a loss. All you have to do is look at specific instances. Look at how each of these examples requires specific mention of the bad situation when the words "I'm sorry" are used:

- I'm sorry you *broke your leg.*
- I'm sorry you *lost the order.*
- I'm sorry you *wrecked the company car.*

Bad situations are commonplace in the insurance industry. And insurance claims that require settlement give us marvelous examples of why we should stay away from "I'm sorry."

For instance, if an agent's client experienced a severe loss to a building from a hailstorm, the client would want to have the damage corrected or receive a reimbursement from the damage. The client wants to hear about a solution, not the accident.

So as the agent we'd focus not on the accident, but on the solution. We wouldn't mention the negative side of the accident and say, "I'm sorry to learn of your disastrous storm damage." Instead we'd avoid the reminder of damage and say, "Expect prompt settlement of your claim."

Death is another classic example where "I'm sorry" should be avoided. We never want to intensify the loss caused by death.

Many think, however, they are sharing sympathy by saying, "I'm sorry to learn of Mary's death in that accident." They shouldn't. By injecting "I'm sorry" into the sentence, they are reinforcing sorrow by reminding another of a tragic situation.

Let's write letters of condolence both with and without "I'm sorry." This is the situation. An employee, Dave, was killed in a tragic automobile accident. As his immediate supervisor, we want to write his wife a letter of sympathy. These next examples show what not to do and what to do:

```
WRONG:

I'm sorry to hear of your husband's death in that tragic
automobile accident. Let me extend my condolences.
```

First, the apology immediately reminds the wife of the death and accident, the bad news. Then "condolences" is used. That word is never friendly.

Following is the right way:

> It was an honor to count Dave as a friend. He was
> special. Somehow he always made the difficult look
> easy. His recommendations always seemed to be right
> on the money, and his sense of humor was truly a
> breath of fresh air around here. We'll certainly
> miss him.
>
> You and your family must have been very proud of
> him. I know we were.

We put the wife first and made no mention of bad news. If we were in her shoes, what would we want to hear? Certainly we would want to avoid the reminder of the death and accident. We would want to hear about what a fine person Dave was or what he contributed at the office. This example turns sorrow into a positive remembrance.

The second paragraph reinforces the positive things Dave did. It wraps up a wonderful letter of sympathy.

This second note created a valued remembrance for the wife. Why? Because it used the personal touch like Dave's sense of humor. You too should add a personal touch whenever you write sympathy notes. By being specific, you create a sense of caring, and caring is why you wrote in the first place.

Now let's look at customer service. A customer made two trips to your store one afternoon. In both situations the customer received discourteous service from two separate employees. The customer has written you about the incidents, returned her credit card, and announced she will not return to your store. What do you write?

The first paragraph sets the tone for the entire letter. Here's a reply we *shouldn't* use. Why? Because it uses "I'm sorry," words that remind the customer of the discourteous service and the reason she left:

> We can't tell you how sorry we are to learn of the discourtesy
> shown you recently by two of our employees. Let us assure you
> there will be no further annoyances.

1. First sentence: The apology forces the store manager to bring up the specific incident. Rather than downplay the incident, the letter immediately reminds the customer why she left in the first place. In effect, this sentence reinforces the customer's dissatisfaction.

2. Second sentence: In an attempt to suggest a solution, the sentence compounds the customer's dissatisfaction with the word "annoyances."
   CONCLUSION: The customer won't return.

Now let's take an approach that skirts the dissatisfaction and puts the customer in a position of feeling good about herself. And by doing this we increase the odds that she will feel good about us. Notice there is no mention of "I'm sorry."

```
You're absolutely right. You deserve prompt and courteous ser-
vice every time you visit _____. Thanks for letting us
know of the service situation. You did us a favor.
```

1. First sentence: Everyone likes to be told they are right. This sentence lets the customer know immediately to expect a friendly letter. With this language we hope defenses will be let down.

2. Second sentence: We're stating a fact our customer certainly agrees with. We're planting a seed that says yes about our store.

3. Third sentence: This sentence expresses appreciation, not apology. We're continuing our positive tone.

4. Fourth sentence: We've turned the complaint around and told the customer, "You're special."
   CONCLUSION: The customer's anger should be neutralized.

By neutralizing the anger, we can then try and create a more positive attitude by explaining corrective action like:

SKIPPING APOLOGIES

```
I've talked with the sales people and stressed the
importance of courtesy. I can assure you I did most
of the talking.

And here's how you helped us. Because of your
comments, we've increased our courtesy training for
all employees, even those who work in the back
offices. Our break areas will have signs that
remind us of the importance of service and how
customers pay our salary. And we plan to have
periodic review on our service efforts.
```

Now with the anger neutralized, we can work on getting the customer back. Then we might continue:

```
You've helped us focus on customer service. Now let
us help you come back to _____. Enclosed is a
15% discount coupon for you on your next visit to
_____. Take advantage of the discount. You'll
get some spectacular savings. (We're having our
fall sale next week.)

You've been a super customer in the past. We'd like
to keep it that way.

COME BACK TO THE SERVICE YOU EXPECT . . .

P.S. Enclosed is an application for a new charge
```

```
with us. Complete it and bring it with you to
_____. Then say, "I'll charge it." Your
account will be instantly reinstated.
```

This letter succeeds, because the first paragraph set the tone for the entire letter. Rather than stirring up previous anger with "I'm sorry," we started on a positive note that set the stage for getting the customer to return.

MORAL: Create remembrances or goodwill, not reminders.

AVOIDING APOLOGIES IN SITUATIONS YOU CAN'T CONTROL

If your neighbor's house burned, did you cause the fire? If your co-worker failed to get a promotion, are you the reason? If another department in your company made a mistake in a shipping order, did you cause the mistake?

Each of these situations states a problem that you had nothing to do with. But by apologizing, you're saying "I'm sorry" for something you weren't involved in, something you had no control over. Why apologize for something you didn't do?

Many times we say "I'm sorry" in a situation we weren't involved in. Then by apologizing, somehow we think everything will be all right. We're off the hook. Perhaps. But bite your tongue in those instances and don't say "I'm sorry." Look for a better way to approach the situation. Why apologize and say "I'm sorry" when you weren't involved or at fault?

This next example could be a typical situation where we might be tempted to say "I'm sorry." Don't. Rather, keep two things in mind. First, don't apologize for something you had nothing to do with. Second, craft the letter on a friendly note so the reader feels good about what you write.

Here's an example. Carl, our subordinate, was injured and will be out for about three months. We want to write him a get-well note. What do we write?

Two letters follow. The first is a poor example that apologizes even though we weren't involved in the accident. The second example injects positive flavor. After each, an explanation follows:

```
WRONG:

I'm sorry to learn of your accident, Carl. Because of your
mishap, you'll probably be absent from work for three months.
We'll try to get along without you.
```

In the first sentence we're apologizing for something we had nothing to do with. And by apologizing we're reminding Carl of the accident. The explanation in the second sentence again reminds Carl of the accident. The last sentence is a good one. It lets Carl know he's important to the operation.

Following is the right way:

WE MISS YOU, CARL!

I wish you were here, Carl. You're a real asset to
our operation. Your contributions will certainly be
missed.

Good luck with your recovery. We look forward to
your speedy return.

In the first paragraph, the first sentence uses positive language. The second sentence puts Carl first and stresses his importance at work. The last sentence reinforces Carl's value. There's not even a hint of anything negative in these sentences.

In the second paragraph, the first sentence looks to the future and makes no mention of absence of time. The second sentence again looks to the future and adds the thought Carl is wanted. Think about the "wanting" comment. All of us like to feel we're wanted.

Humor is another way to show you care without saying "I'm sorry." Here's a story that actually happened.

Sue Stevens is a Lifestyle writer for the Arlington Texas News. She had been in the hospital recovering from surgery and received a few get-well cards each day. One caught her attention and prompted her to write this as a lifestyle article in the paper:

So the other day I was opening my cards and took one out that said, "Congratulations on your Bar Mitzvah." Thinking the mailman had put the envelope in my box erroneously, I didn't open the card and started to put it back in the envelope—which was addressed to me.

So I opened the card. In addition to the printed message was this note:

I didn't like any of the get-well cards and didn't
think you would either. So happy bar mitzvah and
come back to work soon . . . . please! We miss you.
Love, Roy.

Roy Maynard. Our city reporter.

Then Sue continued her article and expressed this comment about the note:

I've always heard laughter is the best medicine, but I'm not real sure that applies when you have stitches down your whole stomach. But if the laughter hurt my stomach, it warmed my heart.

Her reaction shows why Roy's card is pure dynamite. And that's easy to understand.

Rather than say "I'm sorry" and apologize for a hospital stay he had no control over, Roy expressed the unexpected and delivered a powerful message.

When you write a get-well letter or note, consider humor, not apologies. Humor will make both you and the other person feel great.

Let's look at another area where accidents are routine—the insurance industry. Insurance agents constantly face accidents. In fact, some agents probably feel they should apologize after every accident, thinking the apology will make their clients feel better. It doesn't, and they shouldn't. The agent's job is to correct unfortunate accidents, not to apologize. Agents are dealers in goodwill, not apologies.

For instance, if an accident happens that's covered by insurance, the agent should say something that softens the blow and leaves out "I'm sorry." These examples speak for themselves:

```
WRONG: I'm sorry the repairs caused the accident.
RIGHT: You'll get prompt satisfaction.

WRONG: I'm sorry to learn of Tom's death.
RIGHT: Tom truly was a friend.

WRONG: I'm sorry the accident caused you inconvenience.
RIGHT: You've got it. The entire claim was approved.
```

When we can't control an accident or mistake, let's not apologize. Say what you can do, not what you didn't do.

MORAL: If you aren't at fault, *don't apologize.*

SUMMARY

Never write "I'm sorry" in any letter. These words leave a bad taste in readers' mouths.

1. Why you omit "I'm sorry" in any letter:

    a. To avoid its negative tone.

    b. To avoid reminding others of bad situations or disappointments.

    c. To avoid apologies in situations where you weren't at fault.

2. The alternatives or solutions to "I'm sorry."

    a. Replace those words with positive language like "I wish" or "I wanted."

    b. Create goodwill or remembrances, not reminders.

    c. Never apologize for what you can't control. Instead, create positive language that emphasizes solutions. That way, you say what you can do, not what you can't do.

CHAPTER FOUR

THE "YES" PLAN

Learn how to create goodwill letters others will remember as polished gems. By identifying a letter as a yes letter, you're ready to write some of the most powerful letters you will ever write. The "Yes Plan" helps you present that powerful message.

```
You won first prize.

You received the order.

You did a terrific job.
```

Everyone loves "yes" comments like these. Oh, the word *yes* isn't there, but it might as well be. Those comments create exciting feelings. To experience them all you have to do is picture yourself in each of the situations.

If you entered a sweepstakes and then heard, "You won first prize," you'd explode with excitement. If you had worked hours on a large equipment contract and then heard, "You received the order," you'd grin and emphatically say, "All right!" And if you helped your boss with a difficult assignment and then heard, "You did a terrific job," you'd be filled with satisfaction.

These examples tell a story. "Yes" gives magical tone without any effort. And that's a tip-off. "Yes" can help us write some of the most powerful letters we'll ever write, and the implications are staggering. In fact, a carefully crafted "yes" letter can produce spectacular results.

For instance, by saying yes to others, you create valuable goodwill. By developing contacts through "yes" letters, you may encourage others to suggest your company's products or services. And by reinforcing excellent performance, you can expect equally good or better performance from people you work with.

And when it comes to reinforcing excellent behavior, the *One-Minute Manager* knows the power of positive language. To create positive results, author Ken Blanchard said, "Help people reach their full potential. Catch them doing something right."[1]

But let's do more than just catch someone doing something right. Let's shift the positive response and make it even more positive. Let's make that "A" response an "A+." Let's make the impact of yes even stronger on friends, customers, and clients.

Here's how we create that added strength in a letter. We add a fresh dimension that shows how to catch someone doing something right. That fresh dimension is the plan of attack, the yes plan. The yes plan, in turn, lets us focus the power of yes when we write a letter. Here are six steps that show how the yes plan works:

1. Identify your letter.

2. Come to the point immediately with a creative substitution.

3. In the first paragraph, reinforce the salutation's message.

4. Use the letter body to add details that reinforce yes.

5. In the last paragraph, reinforce yes and then look to the future.

6. Use a creative substitution for the complimentary close.

Now let's explore how these ideas work.

1. Identify your letter.

When you pound a nail into a board, do you use a saw? Of course not. You have already identified the situation and know you need a hammer.

Do the same thing with a "yes" letter. Identify the letter. It's one in which you expect a positive response. In it you might congratulate, say thanks, or agree to a meeting.

The key to identifying the "yes" letter is anticipating how others will feel. Will they be excited? Will they be pleased? Will they feel richer because of the letter? If your answer is yes to any of those questions, you have a "yes" letter.

2. Come to the point immediately with a creative substitution.

Always say the good news first in a creative substitution that replaces the salutation. Then, if possible, couple that message with a first name. For added visual impact, always capitalize the message.

Let me explain. If you ever receive a letter that starts with a salutation like "YOU DID A GREAT JOB, (ADD YOUR FIRST NAME)," you'll be hooked. You will want to continue and read all of the letter. Customers or friends would, too. So use examples like these:

- CONGRATULATIONS, TOM:

- YOU'RE REALLY SPECIAL, MARY:

- YOU MADE THE DIFFERENCE, JOE:

Now let's examine why this approach works. Nothing makes others feel better than to be told good news or a friendly comment immediately. That's a clue for us in any "yes" letter. We come to the point immediately and tell the good news first.

The creative substitution gives us a terrific vehicle with which to do just that. These next examples show the impact of coming to the point in the creative substitution:

A transfer
```
WRONG: Dear Tom:
RIGHT: GET OUT YOUR GOLF CLUBS, TOM . . .
```

A job interview offer
```
WRONG: Dear Donna:
RIGHT: WE LIKE WHAT WE SEE, DONNA:
```

A contract award
```
WRONG: Dear Bill:
RIGHT: BILL, YOU'VE GOT THE CONTRACT:
```

A contribution
```
WRONG: Dear Mr. Giving:
RIGHT: HERE'S OUR CONTRIBUTION, GEORGE:
```

Rather than the bland approach of tradition, we're injecting a fresh way of handling how we start a letter. And that new way gives us a difference that creates an even stronger response. We're on our way to writing a powerful letter.

3. In the first paragraph, reinforce the salutation's message.
Add supporting comments in the opening paragraph. Your salutation already makes someone feel terrific. Now make them feel really terrific by continuing your comments. Do that by expanding the initial message of the creative substitution.

You'll find that the creative substitution focuses your message so the first paragraph is easy to write. After all, it's just an extension of what you've already said.

These next examples show the reinforcing, opening paragraph coupled with the creative substitutions listed in the previous step. Notice how the come-to-the-point language in the creative substitutions becomes even stronger with reinforcing, first paragraph language:

A transfer
```
GET OUT YOUR GOLF CLUBS, TOM . . .

You should have been here yesterday. We've got catching up to
do, especially on the golf course.
```

A job interview offer
```
WE LIKE WHAT WE SEE, DONNA:

We're looking for an outstanding chemical engineer. Your
resume suggests you may be the one to fill the job.
```

A contract award
```
BILL, YOU GOT THE CONTRACT:

Your bid coupled with your firm's outstanding reputation for
service made our decision easy. Yes, we want you to have the
advertising contract.
```

A contribution
```
HERE'S OUR CONTRIBUTION, GEORGE:

Enclosed is a $10,000 check. We're glad to help.
```

4. Use the letter body to add details that reinforce "yes."
When people compliment us or say nice things, we never want them to stop. A "yes" letter should work the same way. Since you know the specifics of why the other person is special, tell him or her. Use necessary details and supporting information.

Then that paragraph or paragraphs in the body of the letter give credence to what you've already said. You're supporting your message. You're telling why the other person is special. You're making that other person feel important.

These next paragraphs continue the previous examples and expand earlier positive comments. They add needed details that make the letters come alive.

A transfer
```
It's been a long time since we worked together on a project.
But I can still remember the Smith account. Was our work good
or what?
```

A job interview offer
```
You captured our attention when you were responsible for coor-
dinating a multi-million dollar plant contract. In fact, all
your credentials jumped at us.
```

A contract award
```
You told me to expect creative work. You've already given me
creative suggestions for layout, language, and color choice on
our new ad. I like what you're doing and how you can help us.
```

A contribution
```
Your cancer research is second to none. Your effort is helping
all of us.
```

When you write the body of the "yes" letter, keep in mind that you're the person who knows why you are writing and why the other person is special. So don't be guilty of just saying "yes." Include detail.

For instance, when you assemble a toy for your child, you expect the youngster will enjoy the toy. To help get that enjoyment, you include all the toy's parts. Including the detail in a "yes" letter is like including all the parts.

The point—strengthen the nice comments you made initially in the opening paragraph. Put the reader first by adding to what you've already said. Use the letter's body to reinforce the positive impression someone should already have.

5. In the last paragraph, reinforce "yes" and then look to the future.
That last paragraph starts by reinforcing what you wrote earlier and recalls the good news.

In effect, you recap what makes the person special and continue the glowing comments.

Then the last sentence of that last paragraph looks to the future to suggest further positive performance. That final comment helps maintain or improve goodwill, continue past behavior, or encourage favorable action.

This final paragraph summarizes what you've already said and then adds what you would like to continue. In effect, you restate the good news and then look to the future. So your final paragraph uses language like this:

A transfer
```
You'll be here shortly, and we'll get the chance to work
together again. Tom, I look forward to that.
```

A job interview offer
```
Donna, your employment history tells about a terrific career.
We'd like to hear more of it. I'll call you Thursday, January
12, to set up an interview. I look forward to that.
```

A contract award
```
Bill, you impressed us with your ability to understand our
business. We haven't worked together before, but I know I'll
be saying, "It's been good doing business with you. Keep up
the fine work."
```

A contribution
```
We're proud of your organization's research efforts. George,
I'm glad we can do our part. Keep up the fine work.
```

Notice these examples use "keep up" or "I look forward to" to look to the future. Those words fit most "yes" letters. So keep them in mind when you are finishing your letter, and use them to look to the future.

Notice also that those ending paragraphs all use the word "I." Whoever said to avoid that word in all letters was wrong. When you're writing a friendly letter, the other person often expects you to include the pronoun "I." It adds a friendly touch to your message.

Finally, notice that these examples all use a first name. Use a first name, if possible, in the last paragraph to add a friendly touch. Generally, though, use it only in the last paragraph. More frequent use is almost too much for this kind of letter.

6. Use a creative substitution for the complimentary close.
The complimentary close completes your letter. Rather than the boring tradition of "Sincerely" or "Yours truly," take advantage of a creative substitution. Use this fresh approach to inject friendliness and spice up the close of your letter.

Then by using the creative substitution, you'll have fun thinking up thoughts and ideas that continue your friendly letter.

Your tone throughout is positive. Maintain it in the complimentary close. It's your last thought. These creative substitutions again continue the earlier examples:

A transfer
```
WRONG: Best regards,
RIGHT: BRING YOUR CLUBS . . .
```

A job interview offer
```
WRONG: Sincerely,
RIGHT: LET'S GET TOGETHER . . .
```

A contract award
```
WRONG: Yours truly,
RIGHT: SEE YOU NEXT WEEK . . .
```

A contribution
```
WRONG: Respectfully,
RIGHT: HAVE A WINNING DAY,
```

Further "yes" plan discussion
We've looked at the steps of the yes plan. Now let's look at a "yes" letter and the unsolicited response it got.

Here's a letter I wrote to an Insurance Health Claims Group for a former employer. The Group was doing a fine job handling claims for the company. We wanted the good behavior to continue. To reinforce this good behavior and create goodwill, the situation called for a "yes" letter. Here's what was sent:

"YES" PLAN

```
Supervisor

Group Health Claims

YOU'VE BEEN A BIG HELP, MR. _____:

You and your people have done a fine job in
handling our claims for our division. Thank you.

For the most part, claims have been handled
efficiently and promptly. While there have been
some delays, many were caused by misunderstandings
by our employees, and that's what you have helped
us smooth out.

I know your job of handling these claims must be
difficult at times and yet rewarding knowing that
people are receiving proper benefits.

Please pass on to your people that we appreciate
the work you are doing for us. Thanks for your
help. Keep up your fine job.
```

While addressed to an immediate supervisor, this "yes" letter went beyond him to a vice-president. The vice-president liked what he read. This was his answer:

Your August 7, letter to Mr. _____ has been referred to me and, needless to say, I was extremely pleased to read the very complimentary remarks you had made with respect to our claims service.

In our line of business, which is essentially of a service nature, we are accustomed to receiving complaints whenever mistakes in claim payments are made or when delays in payment occur. It is most unusual for our policyholders to compliment us on a job well done and for this reason, your kind comments are more than appreciated. We hope in the future that our claim service will continue to be satisfactory in all respects.

Vice President

GROUP INSURANCE AND PENSIONS

After examining this example, you probably agree that "yes" letters can cause good things to happen. But if you're looking for immediate results, don't expect them. The intent is to make the other person feel good, not to look for any immediate benefits.

Down the road, however, "yes" letters can only pay dividends. And that's easy to understand. Others don't forget nice comments. They remember them. And that should create terrific goodwill that reminds them of how good you and your company are. No guarantee exists, of course, but it can only help.

Unfortunately, many "yes" letters will probably remain unwritten if they are just for goodwill. They're often letters we don't have to write or ones we can put off writing. For example, how often do we write letters, when we don't have to, that say thanks or congratulate someone for outstanding work?

While some people may never write "yes" letters, top managers do. They know "yes" letters jump with opportunity and are necessary. These managers know that a well-written "yes" letter creates powerful goodwill. So they grab "yes" letters rather than ignore them. Be like them. When you have a chance to write a "yes" letter, take it. You can influence others so something good happens.

Here's another benefit. When writing goodwill letters, you'll save time using the yes plan's steps. You'll find that "yes" letters become routine, not because the letters are routine, but because the yes plan's steps are routine. Translation: You'll write "yes" letters more frequently, because you won't have to spend so much time on them.

With the positive tone of a "yes" letter, you create responses that favorably affect you and your company. AT&T says, "Reach out and touch someone." A "yes" letter not only reaches out and touches someone, it gives a warm hug, too.

SUMMARY

1. Identify the letter as a "yes" letter.

2. Come to the point immediately and always tell the good news in a creative substitution that replaces the salutation.

3. In the opening paragraph, reinforce the good news in the creative substitution.

4. In the letter's body, follow with necessary details and supporting information that reinforces the yes.

5. At the start of the last paragraph, use a friendly tone that continues to reinforce the yes. Then the last sentence of that paragraph looks to the future and suggests positive results.

6. Replace the complimentary close with a creative substitution that ends on a friendly note.

COMBINED EXAMPLES OF CHAPTER LETTERS

1. A transfer

```
"YES" PLAN
```

GET OUT YOUR GOLF CLUBS, TOM . . .

You should have been here yesterday. We've got catching up to do, especially on the golf course.

It's been a long time since we worked together on a project. But I can still remember the Smith account. Was our work good or what?

You'll be here shortly, and we'll get the chance to work together again. Tom, I look forward to that.

BRING YOUR CLUBS . . . .

2. A job interview offer

```
"YES" PLAN
```

WE LIKE WHAT WE SEE, DONNA:

We're looking for an outstanding chemical engineer. Your resume suggests you may be the one to fill the job.

You captured our attention when you were responsible for coordinating a multi-million dollar plant contract. In fact, all your credentials jumped at us.

Donna, your employment history tells about a terrific career. We'd like to hear more of it. I'll call you <u>Thursday, January 12</u>, to set up an interview. I look forward to that.

LET'S GET TOGETHER . . . .

3. A contract award

"YES" PLAN

BILL, YOU'VE GOT THE CONTRACT:

Your bid coupled with your firm's outstanding reputation for service made our decision easy. Yes, we want you to have the advertising contract.

You told me to expect creative work. You've already given me creative suggestions for layout, language, and color choice on our new ad. Yes, I like what you're doing and how you can help us.

Bill, you impressed us with your ability to understand our business. We haven't worked together before, but I know I'll be saying, "It's been good doing business with you. Keep up the fine work."

SEE YOU NEXT WEEK . . . .

4. A donation

"YES" PLAN

HERE'S OUR CONTRIBUTION, GEORGE:

Enclosed is a $10,000 check. We're glad to help.

Your cancer research is second to none. Your effort is helping all of us.

We're proud of your organization's research efforts. George, I'm glad we can do our part. Keep up the fine work.

HAVE A WINNING DAY,

GRANTING CREDIT AND SENDING A CREDIT CARD

SITUATION: Ms. Smith has applied for a credit card at your retail store. She's been approved. Since granting credit is routine, it's important to send the credit card with a letter that is not routine.

NEXT TIME SAY, "CHARGE IT," MS. SMITH!

Ms. Smith, you've been approved for a credit card at
_____. Your credit card is enclosed. Welcome to shopping
at _____.

With your new credit card you'll not only like the convenience, you'll save money, too. As a new credit-card holder, you're entitled to a 15% discount on your next credit-card purchase. Just bring this letter with you and say, "Charge it." The salesperson will gladly take 15% off the price.

This purchase price applies to all sales items. In fact, you may want to take advantage of our upcoming fall sale. Items throughout our stores will be discounted 25%. You'd save an additional 15% with your first credit card purchase.

It's a treat having you as a new customer. We look forward to serving you.

ENJOY SHOPPING AT _____ . . . .

Analysis of the Letter

- The creative substitution lets customers know what they want to hear and uses a fun message.

- The first paragraph reinforces the first impression and tells Ms. Smith she's approved.

- The second paragraph explains a money saving discount.

- The third paragraph gives a specific time to use the card and suggests added savings, something we're all interested in.

- The last paragraph ends with a look to the future.

- The creative substitution plants a seed to shop and suggests enjoyment. "Sincerely" doesn't do that.

CONGRATULATIONS FOR A PROMOTION

SITUATION: A friend, Wayne Winner, recently received a promotion to Vice President, Sales. He works for a large firm that buys large quantities of your widgets. You want to congratulate him, since you've been friends for over 11 years.

IS IT TRUE YOU'VE GOT THE CORNER OFFICE NOW, WAYNE?

Congratulations on your promotion to Vice President, Sales. You certainly earned it.

I just knew your new position was coming. Whenever I saw you at Kiwanis or at our professional meetings, you told me about the sales results you've helped generate. Those comments let me know what a terrific job you were doing.

Wayne, you've been a real asset for your company. They've got a talent they're lucky to have. Keep up your fine work.

LET'S DO LUNCH . . . .

Analysis of the Letter

- The salutation starts with a fun comment that let's Wayne know he's in for a friendly letter.

- The first paragraph amplifies the salutation and comes right to the point.

- The next paragraph gives specifics and brings the message into focus.

- The last paragraph strengthens the earlier comments and looks to the future. Notice nothing is said about doing business with Wayne's company. In a "yes" letter that says thanks or that congratulates, the letter's purpose is to create goodwill, not to make a sales message.

- The complimentary close ends with a fun message and will probably cause Wayne to call.

CHAPTER FIVE

THE "NO" PLAN

Ouch! These are the hardest letters to write. Learn writing techniques that take the sting out of no and reduce your writing struggle, too.

"I'd rather walk ten miles than write that letter!"

"Am I glad Joe has to write that letter. That is one job I sure want someone else to have."

These comments are common when we have a "no" letter to write. And because saying "no" is always difficult, "no" letters require special effort. No one wants to tell anyone bad news.

Saying yes is easy, but many times saying no isn't. For instance, you may be the one who must deny credit to a longstanding customer, so you better know what you're doing. The sloppy use of "no" can cost you that customer.

While no prescription exists for getting the reader to agree with the bad news, you can write a "no" letter that makes the bad news easier to digest, the bitter pill easier to swallow. I suggest the "no" plan.

The "no" plan gives you a plan of action that generates confidence. With it, you know what you are going to write so you improve your effectiveness and save valuable time. It's like a road map that helps you get to your destination efficiently and quickly.

Here are the steps in the "no" plan:

1. Identify the letter as a "no" letter.

2. Omit the salutation.

3. Start with a buffer paragraph.

4. Tell why.

5. Then say no and say it positively.

6. Be pleasant or encouraging in the last paragraph.

7. Omit the complimentary close.

We now have a plan of action. But like a growing plant, we need to see the ideas of the plan develop. So let's start with a "no" letter and use the "no" plan to develop or, in this case, write a denial to a recommendation:

"NO" PLAN

```
Your recommendation to increase the car fleet was
well thought out. It made sense.

Unfortunately profits are down and expenses must be
cut back. For these reasons, the recommendation
must be denied.

Your work on this recommendation was good, John.
Keep up the fine effort and keep those
recommendations coming.
```

Even though no is said, this letter takes advantage of a positive tone and employs that tone to leave, at least, a neutral feeling. You should do the same. As we progress through this chapter, we'll explore how to develop letters like this recommendation denial. We'll discuss the importance of an effective "no."

When I was in business school, I wish I had realized the importance of an effective "no" letter. All students were required to take a course in letter writing. Like many students, I treated the course indifferently, as something "required." Besides, I thought I already knew how to write. Was that a mistake!

Recently, I went through my college text and realized the course had real meat on the importance of "no." Here are some replies to "no" letters I found:

```
My first reaction when I read your refusal (of a discount) was
to ride off in a cloud of dust and take my business somewhere
else. But since thinking it over, I have decided to place my
order with you anyway. You can credit for this the staff of
psychologists you hire to write for you.[1]
```

• • •

```
No one has ever said no to me before and made me like it.[2]
```

• • •

```
If more people would write as you do, there would be a lot less
criticism directed toward the large corporations.[3]
```

These replies demonstrate the importance of an effective "no." Now let's examine the steps in the "no" plan to help you write an effective "no." Here's how the "no" plan works.

1. IDENTIFY THE LETTER AS A "NO" LETTER

Our experience helps us identify the items we need. We also draw on our experience when we write a no or denial. That experience helps us identify a possible negative response. These situations could include:

- Credit denial.

- Job application denial.

- Refusal to grant claim damages.

Then after identifying the situation, we're ready to take the bite out of "no" and use the steps of the "no" plan.

How you write "no" differs dramatically from how you write "yes." With "yes" you come right to the point. With "no" you ease into the negative answer. So anytime you're writing bad news, think red flag; think "this letter requires special treatment;" think of the "no" plan.

2. OMIT THE SALUTATION

In any "no" letter always drop the salutation and go directly from the inside address to the body of the letter. Here's why.

First, "Dear" anybody never makes sense. So that's out.

Second, a creative substitution suggests friendliness and a possible friendly answer. That friendliness can be a turn off when "no" is said.

And last, "no" should be simple. A salutation may not seem like much, but it requires a name. In the denial sentence, we intentionally try to stay away from names or pronouns to keep "no" impersonal. Let's be impersonal in the salutation, too. Drop the salutation and any reference to a name.

3. START WITH A BUFFER PARAGRAPH

Never say "no" in the first paragraph. By saying "no" first, you can expect a negative response and a strong reaction against you. The immediate "no" just reinforces any negative response.

Instead, start with a buffer paragraph that helps drop the other person's defenses. You create that buffer by using friendly language that projects interest in the other person. These next examples show how an immediate "no" ruffles feathers and then how a buffer defuses the same situation.

Here's an incident that could happen in any office. Suppose you need a report typed and ask Susan, a secretary who works for four people, to type it. If she answers, "I can't do it," you immediately react negatively, feel like you are on the defensive, and must justify your request.

If, however, she answers, "I'd be glad to do it. But because there is other work ahead of yours, I won't be able to get to the report for two hours."

That answer starts with the buffer, "I'd be glad to do it." That language should calm you, because it doesn't put you on the defensive like a "no" would. Unless your project is urgent, you are probably satisfied. The secretary's diplomacy eases your stress to get the job done. It takes the hurt out of "no."

Here's an easy way to understand why the secretary's buffer and all buffers work. Compare the buffer thought to an arm that deflects a punch to a boxer's face. Unlike a direct hit to the face, a deflected punch lacks sting. Like the arm that slows a punch, the buffer thought slows the sting of "no."

Now that we've talked about the importance of the buffer before "no," we need some buffer ideas, some cookies to fill the cookie jar. And we have some; they're all designed to help the reader.

- Complimenting the reader.

- Agreeing with the reader.

- Giving acknowledgment.

- Using a neutral fact.

Complimenting the reader

One effective approach is to compliment the reader. If you intend to say "no," the reader needs relief to keep on. To get that needed relief, use a compliment. The compliment puts the reader at ease, because everyone likes nice comments.

For instance, these nice comments should neutralize negative thoughts:

- "The recommendation, in my opinion, has good points."

- "The computer program looks like a good one."

- "Please accept my compliments on your interest in auto safety. I wish more people would express your feelings."

Never, however, abuse the compliment so it suggests a "yes" answer. Suggesting "yes" and then saying "no" often ignites ill will. You avoid the "yes" suggestion by using opinions like "I think" or "It looks" and hedging language like "could," "might," or "may." The advantage—the opinions and hedging language weaken any comments, so you never commit yourself or your company.

```
WRONG: We can help.
RIGHT: I thought we could help.

WRONG: Your proposal is good. It's the sort of thing we're al-
       ways interested in.
RIGHT: Your proposal looks good. It's the sort of thing we
       might be interested in.
```

Here's a "no" letter that compliments the reader about the convention program that an environmental association is presenting. Joe Disposable, an expert on recycling techniques, has been asked to speak at the association's convention but is unable to. He has a conflict in his speaking schedule. This is his answer:

```
Your convention sounds exciting. Hats off to your
planning.

I wish I could join you at the convention. From
what you said, it promises to be a good one. But I
have a conflict. I'll be speaking to a client June
3-5. For this reason, the speaking engagement must
be turned down.

I'll be thinking of you, however, and what you are
doing. Good luck with your convention.
```

Agreeing with the reader

In another buffer approach, agree with something the reader said. Your recognition helps the other person feel important. And even though you eventually say "no," the dignity of initial agreement has the effect of helping the reader. Besides, when "no" is said, readers need all the help they can get.

This next letter is a book proposal rejection from a publisher. The editor agrees with ideas in it but has decided against publishing it.

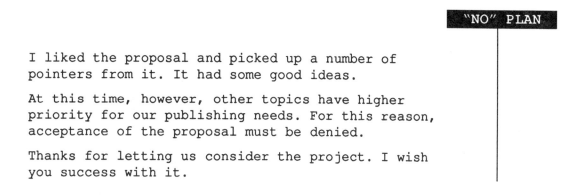

```
I liked the proposal and picked up a number of
pointers from it. It had some good ideas.

At this time, however, other topics have higher
priority for our publishing needs. For this reason,
acceptance of the proposal must be denied.

Thanks for letting us consider the project. I wish
you success with it.
```

Showing acknowledgment

Another effective buffer briefly states that the reader's proposal received consideration. After putting substantial effort into a project or recommendation, people like to be told their proposal received attention. And even if "no" is said, acknowledgment may be all that is necessary to satisfy readers.

So if you are reviewing a project that appears to require extra effort, mention that you gave the project a serious look-see:

- "The research on *Parliamentary Procedure in Business* showed."

- "The recommendation was well thought out and was easy to follow."

Here's a job application denial letter that shows the applicant's resume received consideration:

> When reviewing your resume, it was apparent that a great deal of effort went into it. Thank you for considering XYZ Corporation.
>
> Right now staff requirements are full. In fact, a new hand was hired last week. Because no positions are available, your application for employment must be denied.
>
> You have excellent work experience. Someone will like what you have to offer. Good luck in your job search.

Using a neutral fact

Another buffer technique uses a neutral fact, a fact that creates common ground with the reader. This neutral fact, one with universal appeal like health, pride, or making money, provides an important buffer before the denial.

So use a neutral fact that directs itself at the reader's interest. It can help you disarm a negative response and turn a possible negative reaction into one that is at least neutral or even better, positive.

Neutral facts are broad general statements that cover a common interest. That common interest helps develop a meeting of the minds or an agreement. That agreement, in turn, eliminates conflict or any combative flavor that a "no" situation may create. Here are examples:

- "Successful sales effort and motivation are always important."

- "Everyone should be careful about diets."

- "The budget is a concern of us all."

To get a handle on this approach, broad statements are not enough. We need an example.

A training firm has been putting on a program for your company for ten years, and your people have received valuable training from them. The economics of your company has changed, however, and these training programs must be postponed. You must write the training firm a letter that creates goodwill and says "no" at the same time.

You start with a neutral statement that disarms any negative reaction. Here's your letter.

> Better sales prospecting work is something all industries need. I think everyone can use help in this area. In fact, you've been a big help to us in the past.
>
> But because of our reorganization and because available funds for outside training programs are limited now, any sales training course must be

```
postponed.

Our situation may change at the end of the year.
Contact us in early December, Tom. We'll have a
better picture of what we can do.
```

4. TELL THE WHY

After calming the reader with a buffer, the next step in the "no" plan reviews the facts and gives believable reasons for the disappointing news. You explain why the reader is being turned down. Without an explanation, "no" just becomes harder to accept. It's as if you ordered a tenderloin for dinner and got a hamburger. You'd be upset.

When giving instructions, tell why some approach is important. And the why is critical in the "no" letter if you intend to keep goodwill, future sales, contacts, or any number of favorable profit motives.

Also, always remember to give the reason *before* the "no." If you don't, customers or clients might close their minds to any reasonable explanation. You may cause them to stop reading.

Suppose you operate a hotel and have to turn down a banquet room request for a civic organization on a certain date. You certainly want the organization to reconsider you in the future. With no explanation, however, you leave the other party in the cold. And your chance for getting them to use your facility diminishes dramatically. Failure to explain is like giving up.

So tell them why.

"NO" PLAN

```
I wish we could have you at the hotel for your
banquet. With a month's notice I know we could have
gotten together.

Unfortunately, our banquet facilities are already
booked for the date you requested. The hotel's
banquet facility is unavailable on April 10.

Maybe we can get together next year. Meanwhile,
good luck with your banquet room search.
```

With an explanation, the organization understands why they were turned down. The why leaves the door open for them to return.

Remember the why. Pity privates who have to dig holes and then fill them up. Without any explanation *why* they're doing this physical chore, only frustration can result.

5. SAY "NO"

After the buffer and the "why," then say "no." But the "no" plan makes this so-called difficult task of writing "no" an easier one, because you know what you are doing. You write "no," of course, but you write with positive tone.

Writing techniques that minimize the shock of "no"
People don't like to tangle with a rattlesnake, have their cars break down, or face major home expenses. In fact, people don't like trouble. "No" suggests a problem—or at least a conflict. We should try to minimize that problem or conflict.

Writing techniques can help minimize the shock of "no." And while these techniques never make the shock totally disappear, they do reduce the impact of that shock. So let's examine some of those techniques. Here are six:

1. Saying what something is, not what it isn't.

2. Saying what you can do, not what you can't do.

3. Using the subjunctive.

4. Using the passive voice.

5. Avoiding an accusing tone.

6. Avoiding "not."

Say what something is, not what it isn't. When you're seeking a positive answer, you never like to be told negative facts. Even though "no" is the answer, you still want a positive approach. One way for you to create that positive approach is to stress what something is rather than what it is not. This way you deal from strength rather than weakness.

For instance, you want to hear what a gasoline additive does: "It improves performance," not what it doesn't do (guarantee 50 miles per gallon mileage). Other examples follow:

```
WRONG: The warranty does not cover mishandling.
RIGHT: The warranty covers everything but mishandling.

WRONG: The insurance policy does not include wind damage to
       trees around a house.
RIGHT: The insurance policy covers all wind damage to the
       house but excludes fallen trees around the house.
```

Say what you can do, not what you can't do. This positive approach gives a solution rather than an empty "no." You give readers an answer that's not offensive:

```
WRONG: You failed to send us your report, so we cannot . . .
RIGHT: Please send us your report, so we can . . .

WRONG: If you do not complete the form, we cannot . . .
RIGHT: When you complete the form, we will be glad to . . .
```

More important, you may stimulate future sales by saying what you can do. For example, suppose a large retailer has ordered 1,000 shoes, style 101. That line has been discontinued. What do you write?

You wouldn't say, "We can't fill your order." A flat "no" like that is cold and, in effect, says you don't *want* the order.

But you do want the sale. To get that business you say what you can do, not what you can't do. You might then write:

```
Your order for 1,000 shoes, style 101, was
terrific. We certainly appreciate your confidence
in our quality.

I wish the order could be filled, but that line has
been discontinued. We can, however, substitute
style 201.

That shoe is not only similar in quality and
appearance to style 101, but you receive a 10%
discount during its initial offering. So that you
can learn more about this new shoe, a circular on
shoe style 201 is enclosed.

I'll call you on Monday, May 14, about filling your
order. Let's look at style 201 and save you some
money.
```

Think about the power of saying what you can do. You change a no into a possible yes.

Using the subjunctive. To limit shock, use the subjunctive to say no. "If" normally precedes the thought.[4] This technique communicates an element of comfort, because of the positive approach. Just as repeated exercise gives strength to an athlete, so too the subjunctive gives strength to your writing. It's an effective way to say no.

```
WRONG: The policy does not cover floods.
RIGHT: If the policy covered floods, the money would be paid
       promptly.

WRONG: We cannot send you a replacement, because the warranty
       does not cover the fuel pump.
RIGHT: If the warranty covered the fuel pump, a replacement
       would have been sent.
```

Using the passive voice. Another language technique that limits "no" shock is the use of the passive voice—the helping verb "to be" and a verb's past participle.[5] Always use this technique in any denial sentence, because the passive voice is impersonal and divorces specific people from the no. It helps get rid of proper names and pronouns like *I, we, you,* and *your.*

You keep away from poison ivy to avoid the discomfort of a terrible itch. Likewise, when you write *no,* you keep away from the mention of people to separate them from the discomfort of "no." The passive voice lets you use this impersonal approach.

For instance, with the passive voice you can eliminate the personal pronoun *you.* The passive voice also helps you sidestep *I* or *we* and avoid putting yourself or your company first. These next examples show how the passive voice eliminates people.

```
WRONG: I must deny your recommendation.
RIGHT: The recommendation is denied.

WRONG: Because the controversy remains unsettled, we must
       postpone your claim.
RIGHT: Because the controversy remains unsettled, the claim
       must be postponed.
```

Avoid an accusing tone. Here's another way to write an effective "no" and make negative tone vanish. When you accuse, you invite trouble. An accusing tone puts readers on the defensive and makes them feel like fools. When readers feel foolish, you lose.

Who wants to be told that he or she made a mistake? Who wants to be abused? No one. Yet that's exactly what we do when we accuse. Study these examples:

```
WRONG: You claimed extensive damage to your transmission.
RIGHT: If it were possible to extend the warranty coverage
       beyond three years, the transmission would be covered.

WRONG: According to you, the items sent were inferior.
RIGHT: Please look at the catalogue specifications on page 31.
       You'll find that the widget specifications were met.

WRONG: You failed to give us the necessary documents.
RIGHT: To help us give you quicker service, please send us a
       copy of the death certificate. We can get right on your
       claim.
```

Avoiding not. Also avoid *not* in any denial. *Not* definitely says "no," but this three-letter word is negative rather than positive. It's harsh. By avoiding *not*, we help take the harshness out of a denial.

So rather than couple a verb with *not*, use a verb that eliminates *not*:

```
WRONG: The company cannot give you any credit for your claim.
RIGHT: The claim is denied.

WRONG: We will not approve the service.
RIGHT: The service is denied.
```

And if a positive verb eludes you, use a negative verb form (like *dislike* rather than *don't like*).

```
WRONG: We cannot allow the reimbursement.
RIGHT: The reimbursement is disallowed.

WRONG: We can't approve the credit.
RIGHT: The credit is disapproved.
```

6. BE PLEASANT WHEN CLOSING
The last part of the "no" plan is the closing paragraph. We've said no. Now we must close.

To be effective, the closing must be pleasant. If ever readers need a pick-me-up, they need one when you tell them no. So you reserve the last paragraph to capture a friendly tone.

You might capture that friendly tone with an encouraging comment that expresses a wish for good luck. You might end with a suggestion that another company could help. Or you might write about a helpful enclosure.

No matter what the approach, however, every denial closing looks at the other's point of view and never reminds the reader of the bad news. When you say no in a letter, you should think about comforting the reader. This means discussing something other than the bad news at the end of a "no" letter.

Earlier I said to avoid pronouns like *you, we,* or *I* when saying no. After the denial, however, personal pronouns or even names may fit better than anything else. The "you" or name gives a personal flavor. The "I" or "we" may give a necessary opinion.

For instance, you might write:

- Your approach was refreshing, John. I think it can work.
  Keep at it.

- I think you have some good thoughts. Keep developing them
  and good luck.

- You have excellent skills. Good luck with your job search.

Like the "yes" plan, the "no" plan looks to the future in the last paragraph. That look to the future provides an element of hope. That hope should be a catalyst that keeps customers.

Retail stores often deny credit to customers. They want these customers, however, to continue to buy from their stores. An effective closing paragraph in a "no" letter helps to do just that.

Here's an example. Charlie Customer has applied for credit and a credit card at your store. His credit record shows failure to pay bills on time. You must write him a letter that refuses credit.

Notice the tone of the last paragraph in this next letter. It offers hope (changing circumstances) and encourages Charlie to remain as a customer (mailing list).

"NO" PLAN

You pleased us when you applied for credit at
_____. Your interest is appreciated. Thank you.

If it were possible to extend credit, approval would
be given. Your credit history, however, suggests a
better record of paying bills is needed. For this
reason, the credit request is denied.

When conditions change, we welcome the opportunity
to consider a new application. In the meantime,
we've put you on our mailing list to keep you
current on advance sales.

Credit Department Supervisor

What you write last can be indelible and leave its mark. Why not leave a favorable impression?

7. DROP THE COMPLIMENTARY CLOSE

The only reason we use the complimentary close is tradition. Tradition suggests there must be a complimentary close to end a letter.

No! The complimentary close is added baggage when writing "no." If you want something to end the letter, sign your name. The traditional complimentary close is empty and adds nothing to the effectiveness of a denial. End your letter with an encouraging paragraph, not the meaningless complimentary close.

SUMMARY

The "no" plan prepares you to write "no" and gives a step-by-step pattern that helps you know what to say and what not to say. And because you know how to handle "no," you're better able to write an effective "no."

In addition, you save time. With a plan of action you spend less effort thinking about how to write "no." Consequently, you free yourself for more productive work.

1. Identify the letter as a "no" letter.

2. Drop the salutation.

3. Begin with a buffer paragraph.

    a. Compliment the reader.

    b. Agree with the reader.

    c. Show acknowledgment.

    d. Use a neutral fact.

4. Review the facts and give believable reasons for the disappointing answer.

5. Then say "no" and say it positively.

    a. Say what you can do, not what you can't do.

    b. Say what something is rather than what it is not.

    c. Use the subjunctive.

    d. Always say "no" with the passive voice.

    e. Never accuse.

    f. Avoid *not* in any denial.

6. Be pleasant or encouraging in the last paragraph.

7. Drop the complimentary close.

CHAPTER SIX

THANK YOU, USED AND ABUSED

We've been told to use thank you. But we haven't been told how to use these words.

Our mother was right. The words *thank you* are magic. Whenever anyone tells us *thank you,* we feel great. We love these words, because they bring back good memories. No one could change our minds about how special these words are.

Unfortunately, just as we rarely think about breathing, we rarely think about *how* to use *thank you.*

The "thank you approach"

By knowing how to use *thank you,* we have a terrific opportunity to make others feel truly special, because these words fairly scream opportunity. In fact, the proper use of *thank you* is so obvious, it hurts.

What is the proper way? Always praise the deed first and put *thank you* last.

Think about *thank you.* Why do we say it? We say it because someone did something. And because we are thanking for a deed, doesn't it make sense to put the deed first and not *thank you*?

No book taught me how effective *thank you* can be. I learned this from some elementary school students. A number of years ago I gave a talk to a sixth-grade class. The teacher had each student write me a thank-you note. Twenty-six of the students expressed appreciation and wrote something like this:

```
Thank you for your talk. I liked it very much.
```

Two students wrote thoughts like this:

```
Your talk was great. Thank you.
```

When I read those two letters I asked myself, "Why do I like those two best?" After some thought, the difference became apparent. Two students had put me first. While all the students said about the same thing, two had flattered me when they commented first on my talk.

Those two students made me aware of the obvious, something I overlooked even though *thank you* stares me in the face every day. They, in effect, told me to put people first, not *thank you*.

Now let's use the ideas the students gave me and apply them to a situation that may arise anytime. Suppose Paul, a subordinate, prepared an outstanding report on how to reduce inventory costs. You're impressed with it and want to thank Paul for a job well done. You might then say:

```
Thanks for your help, Paul. The inventory report will dramati-
cally improve our profit picture. You did an outstanding job
on it.
```

He'd like that comment. But rather than just express appreciation by putting *thank you* first, let's place the emphasis on Paul and not on *thank you*. Let's shift his expected response from "A" to "A+." Then we would reverse the language and say:

THANK YOU

```
TOP-NOTCH REPORT, PAUL!

You did an outstanding job on the inventory report,
Paul. It will dramatically improve our profit
picture. Thanks for your help.
```

You said the same thing, but in a different order. And with this order change, you stressed Paul and put *thank you* in the background. By putting Paul first, you made him feel important. And anytime you put someone first, that's effective communication.

Reinforcing the deed
One other element exists when we use *thank you*: the why or consequences of the deed.

When others flatter us, we generally don't want them to stop. We want to savor the moment and have them go on and on and on. Why? Because they're making us feel important. If that's so, we'd better further examine *thank you*.

The first thing we do is praise the deed. So far so good. But jumping from the deed to *thank you* overlooks *why* we thank someone. Don't leave out the why. That is the specific that shows we care.

Employees, probably more than anyone else, want to know how they stand. They want specifics when it comes to performance. If they hear they did a good job and get a "thanks" too, they still don't know what made their performance worth of a *thank you*. Tell them. Give them the specifics.

But don't limit your why to employees. Use the why whenever you say *thank you*. Let customers, colleagues, and friends know why their deeds are special. These examples show how the why improves the *thank you*:

```
GOOD:    You did a terrific job. Thanks for your help.
BETTER:  You did a terrific job. Your idea about the insert will
         improve our results. Thanks for your help.

GOOD:    What a great idea. Thanks.
BETTER:  What a great idea. Your THANK YOU APPROACH will give
         me an intangible advantage with customers. Thanks.

GOOD:    The letter opener gift was perfect. Thanks.
BETTER:  The letter opener gift was perfect. I love it. Besides,
         how many people have a customized letter opener with
         their name on it? Thanks.
```

We've just discussed what I call the "Thank-You Approach." Its elements include:

1. Praise the deed first.

2. Tell the consequences or why.

3. Express appreciation last.

Using the "thank-you approach" in opening paragraphs of business letters
Ideally, we should follow the "Thank-You Approach" every time we say *thank you* in a conversation. But because we've learned *thank you* as automatic, sometimes we slip and put it first. And that's easy to understand. In conversations, we rarely have the luxury of planning what we're going to say.

That's not true in a business letter. We do have time to plan what we want to say. So always use the "Thank-You Approach" as the first paragraph in any thank-you letter. Keep these thoughts in mind:

1. You're thanking others for what they did. Always praise their performance first.

2. Remember, when you're flattered you want to know why. Your customers and friends do, too. Give them the reason.

3. Put *thank you* in the last sentence of the paragraph. Never start a thank-you letter with the words *thank you*. By putting *thank you* first, you abuse those words, and they are too valuable a commodity to waste.

Let's now examine the effectiveness of the "Thank-You Approach." This next example shows how the "Thank-You Approach" sparks effectiveness.

Suppose a major supplier has been consistently on time delivering goods to us. Having that reliable source of supply has been important to our firm's success. We want to insure that valuable relationship continues.

Probably the best thing we can do is to maintain personal contact with their people. A letter of thanks can help cement that ongoing relationship.

What would you say if you were assigned the job of saying thanks? Many of us would just express appreciation and write this kind of letter:

```
Thank you for your conscientious effort in keeping an uninter-
```

rupted supply of goods flowing to us. Your effort has helped
our profitability. We certainly appreciate it.

While friendly, that letter includes only appreciation. Here is a neglected opportunity. Using the same situation, let's write a thanks that packs power:

What a difference you make! Your reliability as a supplier has
been fantastic. You certainly make it easy to keep doing business with you. Thanks for your outstanding service.

The point—turn appreciation into an opportunity. Say what makes others feel good. Put *thank you* in the background.

Now let's assume someone gives us a large, new order. Most of us would agree the order requires a *thank you*. For that follow-up, many either use the telephone or write a letter. But what do they say or write? A natural reaction would be to express appreciation and to say *thank you* as:

Thank you for your new order. We really appreciate it.

With a new order we're trying to create goodwill. Instead of a traditional approach that says *thank you* first, let's use the "Thank-You Approach" to thank our customer. Then we would say:

THANK YOU

BETTER PERFORMANCE IS ON THE WAY . . .

You'll like your order selection, Tom. With the new
widgets you can definitely expect improved results.
Thanks for your confidence in the widget's quality
and thanks for your order.

TALK TO YOU SOON!

Now think about people management. When we have a chance to say *thank you*, act like the alert supervisor and grab the "Thank-You Approach." Help maintain performance by making others feel important.

For instance, if a colleague contributes to a recommendation, if one of your sales people helps with a sales promotion, or if a subordinate presents a terrific program, by all means thank them. But praise the deed so you put them first. You might then write:

What terrific ideas you had. Your contribution made it easier
to sell the program to XYZ Corporation. Thanks for your outstanding work.

• • •

That was fine help you gave with the sales promotion. You
really did your homework. Thank you.

· · ·

```
What a terrific approach. You got everyone interested in the
topic. You really made our department look good. Thanks.
```

What to say in the middle paragraphs
The opening paragraph uses the "Thank-You Approach." The next section supports the why and gives specific details, facts, and figures.

With flattery, we like others to continue. That's what the middle of the letter does—gives added strength to the thank-you message. These next examples are middle paragraphs that explain why someone's speech was well received:

```
You covered many items that hit a nerve somewhere. But probab-
ly more than anything, you stressed the importance of self-
help. Significantly, you equated that with common sense. Yes,
we got a powerful message.
```

· · ·

```
A special part of your presentation was your interpretation of A
Midsummers Night's Dream. You had the laughing bug bite us, and
then you kept us laughing with your antics. It was wonderful.
```

· · ·

```
The help you gave me was spectacular. But your executive as-
sistant deserves special recognition. She was always going
that extra mile to ensure we had a good program. You must be
very proud of her.
```

The middle paragraphs let you stand out because you expand the deed with specific details. Those details reinforce the good feeling you've already established in your first paragraph.

Developing closing paragraphs in thank-you letters
The closing paragraph of a letter uses the "Thank-You Approach" too, but with a twist. As the last thought, drop the *thank you* and replace it with a sentence that looks to the future. The last paragraph then follows this pattern:

1. Praise the deed.

2. Give the why.

3. Omit *thank you*.

4. Look to the future.

An ending paragraph would then use language like this:

```
What a wonderful letter you sent me. You made me feel ten feet
tall. I certainly look forward to working with you again.
```

Our initial discussion showed how *thank yous* present us with an opportunity to make others feel special by putting them last. Now, in the closing paragraph, we add to that opportunity by replacing *thank you* with a thought that looks to the future.

Here's why. Saying *thank you* is not enough in the last paragraph. *Thank you* only refers to or mentions the past. These words fail to look to the future. But we want to look to the future. We want to ensure that our relationship continues.

So we use language that looks to the future. With it we help others remember the goodwill our letters generate. In effect, they remember us. That remembering may reinforce previous behavior. It may cement a valuable bond and create goodwill. Or it may mean more business at a later date.

So when your letter says *thank you*, use your last paragraph as an opportunity to reinforce past behavior, create goodwill, or help generate future business. Include a positive look to the future as the last thought. For example:

```
Your ideas and effort were terrific, Mary. Your continuous help
certainly gave us all a lift. Keep up your outstanding work.
```

• • •

```
We couldn't have done it without you. Your contribution helped
us get that timely contract. I look forward to working with
you again.
```

• • •

```
You've been a terrific customer. It's been a pleasure serving
you. We look forward to serving you again.
```

• • •

```
Your excellent effort, I'm sure, will continue. You certainly
made a tremendous impact on us. Keep it up.
```

• • •

```
You provide a valuable service to the community. Others must
enjoy it as much as we do. Keep up that fine work.
```

To further see how the look to the future strengthens our letters, let's go back to that large, new order we talked about earlier. In answering the order request, we used the "Thank-You Approach."

When creating goodwill, though, we want customers to remember us. That means we help them remember with a look to the future. We'd then have a letter with an ending paragraph like this:

```
Working with you has been a treat, Tom. It's been fun watching
your business grow. When you're ready to place another order
for widgets or another one of our products, let me know. I'll
get right on it.
```

The last thought looked to the future and let Tom know how easy it will be to do business with us again. We've helped him remember us and our products. We've created a situation that suggests he do business with us again.

The handwritten thank-you note

When you use handwriting to say *thank you*, it's powerful. Handwriting shouts personal attention. You're hitting a home run by giving your message a personal touch.

Handwritten thank-you cards make sense when you want a short note that just expresses appreciation. They're always friendly, always remembered, and always have impact.

Since we frequently write short thank-you notes, let's discuss tips to help you save time, be consistent, and create a lasting impact.

Here are some guidelines:

1. Include a printed thank you, a message, or corporate name on the front of the card.

2. Be "dearless." Start with a name only or with a short message and name.

3. Either drop the complimentary close or use a brief message as a replacement.

4. Sign only your first name.

First, let's look at the card itself. It can have different printed information and can come in all sizes and shapes.

One I received that reflected variety at its best was from Employers Insurance of Texas. That card was many colored and had *thank yous* plastered all over it. But there was more. *Thank you* was in different fonts, sizes, and directions. Here was a beautiful example of what imagination can do with a card.

All cards, however, are not that elaborate. Some have either *thank you* or the corporate name on the front. Some will have both *thank you* and the corporate name on them. And some cards are just that, postcards with the thank-you message on one side and the address on the other. All of them work, because they have a message that makes the card special.

While size varies, I generally suggest a folded card be 3¼" by 5¼" to 4¼" to 6 ½". For a postcard I suggest a letter-size card.

Let me explain. The reduced size of the folded card forces us to be direct, makes the note short, and prevents long notes that may be hard to read. In effect, the reduced size ensures that our message will have impact.

When saying *thank you* on a postcard, I suggest a letter size because it's difference stands out from the ordinary postcard. And with a letter size, there is no postage surcharge.

For our second guideline, make the acknowledgment "dearless." Use either a name or a short message with a name. "Dear" is unnecessary in a personal note. Just acknowledge with:

- `Jane`
- `Mr. Smith`

- It's perfect, Ed

Third, drop complimentary closes like "Sincerely" and either go directly to the signature or use a short expression.

Generally the complimentary close is unnecessary. Since the intent is friendliness, the message stands on its own. You've already made the other person feel good.

That doesn't mean you can't use a brief creative substitution for the complimentary close. Sometimes you may want to end with a message. When you do, use only brief language with no more than three or four words. These examples give ideas you might use:

- See you Friday.
- Count on me.
- Enjoy.

And last, sign only your first name. The first name ensures a friendly touch. Nothing expresses friendliness more than using your first name.

Here's an example of a short, handwritten thank-you note. Tom helped you with a closing on a home loan. As a real-estate agent, you appreciated the way he speeded up the paperwork for your clients. You might then write this:

THANK YOU

> Tom,
>
> Your experience came through. You whisked my clients through the closing paperwork. Thanks for your super help
>
> Mary

Notice this short note did not look to the future. The purpose here was only acknowledgment. Nothing more was needed. In a short thank-you note, especially handwritten ones, just follow the "Thank-You Approach." Don't worry about looking to the future.

In contrast, looking to the future may fit some short thank-you notes. If the look to the future fits, use it:

THANK YOU

> Carl,
>
> Your presentation sold the idea. Management adopted your program. Thanks for your help. Keep up your good work!
>
> Betty

Thank you abuse in closing paragraphs

```
Thank you in advance for your contribution.
```

No! No! No! Never thank anyone in advance for anything. This language is both presumptuous and unnecessary. Let me explain.

As youngsters we learned the magic of *thank you* when we received something like a cookie from our mom. We learned that *thank you* expressed appreciation. And if we expressed appreciation, good things would probably happen again. For instance, we might get another cookie.

And we learned to continue to say *thank you* as we grew older. When we received a gift, we expressed appreciation. When someone did something for us, we said thanks. We thought of *thank you* as what mother had told us it was: magic.

Unfortunately, *thank you*'s meaning became warped. Some extended *thank you* to include items not yet received. The result? A new meaning. *Thank you* became words that tried to persuade. But all they did was hope. These examples show what I mean:

```
WRONG: Thank you in advance for giving me the $5.00 in your pocket.
TRANSLATION: I hope you'll give me the $5.00 in your pocket.

WRONG: Thank you in advance for your time.
TRANSLATION: I hope you'll give me your time.

WRONG: Thank you in advance for ordering it.
TRANSLATION: I hope you will order it.
```

Okay, if we can't use *thank you* to persuade, what *should* we do? Use action verbs.

Since you want someone to do something, use the strength of persuasive, active verbs like *take, join,* or *give.* And since you expect results, put the power words in the imperative, so you make your sentences orders with an implied "you."

```
WRONG: The widget works. Thank you in advance for your order.
RIGHT: The widget works. Take advantage of its benefits. Use
       the order form and return it in the courtesy envelope.

WRONG: Thank you in advance for joining ABC Association.
RIGHT: The ABC Association makes sense. Join today.

WRONG: Thank you in advance for giving to the United Way.
RIGHT: Help the United Way help others help themselves. Give
       to the United Way.
```

Let's look at a different area now. Often readers have no choice but to follow your request. In those instances don't start with *thank you* as a weak persuader. Instead use the imperative and politely tell them what to do:

```
WRONG: Thank you in advance for completing the color informa-
       tion you failed to include the first time.
```

```
RIGHT:  Please add the color you want and then return your order
        form to us so we can ship your widgets immediately.

WRONG:  Thank you in advance for completing and returning the
        credit application form.
RIGHT:  Please complete and return the credit application form.

WRONG:  Thank you in advance for sending us the three dollars
        for your transcript.
RIGHT:  Please send three dollars for your transcript.
```

The benefits of the "thank-you approach"
First, you will make others feel terrific about what you say or write. These are just some of the reactions I've heard from people who received "Thank-You Approach" letters:

- `You made my day.`
- `It's a treat to count you as a friend.`
- `You were terrific to think of me.`
- `I made it a point to put your letter in my personnel file.`
- `You made me feel special. Thoughtful people like you are a rare commodity.`

These reactions tell a story. You're generating valuable goodwill by using this approach. You're helping others remember you. That remembering may not mean an immediate sale. It may not even mean a sale. But the goodwill you develop should create dividends down the road.

A second benefit—you save time. A good example is when a bride writes thank-you notes for wedding gifts. Those notes must seem endless to her. But by knowing how to handle *thank you*, she has a plan of action. That means she can rattle them off quickly.

In business we are constantly faced with writing thank-you letters and notes. So take advantage of the timesaving plan of action of the "Thank-You Approach." With it you can be certain you'll save time.

The third benefit—you feel great about yourself. Because you know how to make others feel terrific, you know *your* letter will stand out. You'll have the satisfaction and fun of knowing you made a wonderful difference.

SUMMARY

Using *thank you* correctly is like riding a bicycle. Once we learn, we never forget. So when you use the words, never abuse them.

1. How the "Thank-You Approach" works.

   a. Always praise the deed first.

   b. Next, tell them why you are thanking them.

   c. Then put *thank you* last and in the background.

2. Using the "Thank-You Approach" in opening paragraphs.

   a. You're thanking others for what they did. Always praise their performance first.

   b. Remember, after you've praised the deed, your customers and friends want to know why you flattered them. Tell them.

   c. Put *thank you* in the last paragraph. By putting *thank you* first, you miss an opportunity to make these words shout.

3. What to say in the middle paragraph or paragraphs.

   a. Give specific details to expand the why.

   b. Specifics show you care because you're taking added time to say why.

4. Developing closing paragraphs in thank-you letters.

   a. Praise the deed.

   b. Tell the why.

   c. Omit *thank you.*

   d. Replace the *thank you* with a look to the future.

5. The handwritten thank-you note.

   a. Use a card that includes your company name, says *thank you,* or has some message.

   b. Be "dearless." Start with a name or a short message.

   c. Say *thank you.*

   d. Either drop the complimentary close or use a short message as a replacement.

   e. Sign only your first name.

6. Thank you abuse in closing paragraphs.

   a. Never say *thank you* in advance.

   b. Thank you is presumptuous and unnecessary when nothing is received.

7. Benefits of the "Thank-You Approach."

   a. Makes others feel terrific.

   b. Saves time.

   c. Makes you feel good.

THANK-YOU EXERCISES THAT WILL HELP YOUR CREATIVITY

1. A sales representative sent you a gift for your birthday. Write that person a thank-you note.

2. Jo's work on the research project added significantly to your results. As her supervisor, you want to give her recognition and also have your letter included in her personnel file. What do you write?

3. Another company helped you complete a project on time. Write the president of that firm and say thanks.

4. You've just received an unusually large order from an old customer. How are you going to say thanks?

5. Volunteer employees made your corporate fund-raising program a success. As Division Manager, write them and say thanks.

6. A client has been selected the outstanding small business person for the year by the Chamber of Commerce. What will you write?

THANKING A LUNCHEON SPEAKER

SITUATION: A police officer spoke to your civic club about residential security. As program chairman you are to write and thank her for her presentation.

WHAT A HELPFUL TALK, JANET:

Your talk yesterday on residential security was terrific. You captured everyone's attention. Thanks for the information.

You covered dead-bolt locks, adequate lighting, and a number of other items. You must have hit a bunch of hot buttons. But probably more important than anything, you stressed the importance of self-help. Significantly, you equated that with common sense. Yes, we got a powerful message.

You provide a valuable service to the citizens in Middleton. The information can help all of us. Keep up the fine work.

HAVE A TERRIFIC NEW YEAR . . . .

Analysis of the letter

- The creative substitution captures attention.
- Reinforce the situation and then say thanks.
- Give specific details that support the thanks.
- Comment again on the talk's value and then look to the future.
- Use a friendly creative substitution.

THANKING A PROFESSIONAL SPEAKER

SITUATION: Sammy Speaker gave a terrific keynote speech at your national convention. As program chairman, you want to let him know how everyone enjoyed his talk at the convention.

YOU WERE DYNAMITE, SAMMY!!!

When the audience interrupted you umpteen times for applause and laughter, all of us knew what a super talk we were hearing. You certainly started our convention with a bang. Thanks.

I particularly liked your vacation story and all the complications you faced. That story's message helped us remember the importance of planning. In fact, all your personal stories had messages. What can I say? You were terrific.

Sammy, you set a wonderful tone for our convention. I'll bet you've made other audiences feel as good as we did. Keep up your fine work. You did a great job.

YOU'RE A WONDERFUL STORYTELLER . . . .

Analysis of the letter

- Just as a keynote sets the tone for a convention, the salutation sets the tone for a letter. This salutation does just that.

- The first paragraph reinforces the quality of the speech and puts Sammy first.

- The second paragraph goes into the specifics of the talk and gives support to the nice comments in the first paragraph.

- The last paragraph repeats the nice comments and then looks to the future. Sammy will remember this testimonial for a long time.

- The complimentary close caps the friendly letter. Rather than "Sincerely," the creative substitution ends with a powerful message.

CHAPTER SEVEN

PERSUADING TIPS THAT CREATE RESULTS

Learn persuading tips that will help you get ahead and give you an edge on your peers and competitors.

You sold me, Charlie. Let's go to the basketball game.

This example shows that friends persuade, that you don't have to be in sales to sell. Each day we sell our ideas to others. Sometimes we succeed, and sometimes we don't. Why?

Confidence? Who knows. Knowing your audience? Perhaps. Getting attention? Maybe. These ideas could all affect selling. If we had the secret of selling, however, we'd all be millionaires. No magic formula exists.

Just as there are valuable cards in a baseball card collection, there are valuable persuasion ideas for business letters. We'll explore some of those ideas and discuss three concepts that will help you with persuading letters.

1. The AIDA approach.

2. Anticipate what the reader wants to read.

3. Items to avoid.

Now let's examine them.

THE AIDA APPROACH

In any persuading letter, we improve our odds for success by knowing what motivates. That means using motivational ideas psychologists suggest like making money, saving money, attracting the opposite sex, success, and shelter. Other motivational elements exist, of course, but all have one thing in common—they persuade us to do something, to act.

To put those persuading elements into action, we need a plan. I use the AIDA plan, an approach most sales people are familiar with.

A—Win their ATTENTION
I—Arouse their INTERESTS
D—Create a DESIRE
A—Stimulate ACTION or AGREEMENT[1]

Remember, however, the AIDA plan is just a selling approach and not a formula that guarantees instant results. Only people present imaginative ideas; results only come when you put the imaginative ideas to work. Now let's examine the AIDA plan.

Capturing attention
The first sentence is the most important in a persuading letter. It's the one that can either make or break us. Salespeople call this sentence the hook, something to grab the reader. Since we generally expect an indifferent or neutral reaction to a sales letter, we must create a positive opening that catches the reader's attention. Without interest or excitement in the opening, the reader couldn't care less about what we feel is important. We must then find an item of persuasion that arouses curiosity, so readers will want to continue.

Starting with a question is one way to capture this curiosity. Mentally, a question requires an immediate answer. Since you want a positive response, ask an open-ended question that hooks the reader and can't be answered with a simple yes or no. The who, what, where, when, why, and how of journalistic fame work here. Consider the following examples.

- Who works with it?

- What are the options?

- Where are the gurus of gloom now?

- When did the direction change?

- Why do some succeed when they invest their money?

- How many times have people asked, "How can I make this chore easier?"

If, however, you ask a question that is not open-ended, ask only those that have a yes answer. Don't ask one that gives the reader the opportunity to say no. A no puts the reader in a negative frame of mind and makes your effort easy to reject.

These examples show how easily you lose the reader when using questions that people can answer no.

```
Will you join me?
     "No, why should I"

Did you ever win first prize?
     "Of course not. And I never will."

Do you like water polo?
     "No. I don't even know how to swim."
```

A yes answer, however, creates the proper mood for more yes answers. Salespeople certainly know the importance of getting their client or customer to say yes. For instance, if customers say yes, they'll probably continue to say yes, and salespeople improve their chance of closing the sale. So you need to be aware of the power of yes. Here are examples of questions that suggest yes:

- Do you want to cut your heating costs?
- Do you want to improve your investment success?
- Do you want a larger income?

We're on the A-for-attention step, so let's look at another technique to gain attention, the intriguing suggestion. Just as an opening question captures attention, so does an intriguing suggestion. With an intriguing suggestion you want the emotion of your key word or phrase to hit a nerve. If you hit nerves, you hook readers; they want to read on. Here are examples:

- Take a good look at your landscaping and picture how you can make it even better.
- Check the candidates' qualifications and their voting records.

Arousing interest

After securing the reader's attention, carry the attention forward and create interest by answering questions, describing benefits, and supplying statistics. Tell readers what's in it for them, what they'll receive. To do that you stress persuasive elements like cutting costs, increasing profits, helping others, or improving health.

The interest section of any persuading letter plays on the emotions of readers. Here you say what readers will get for their money or efforts. For instance, "A purchase now saves you an additional 20%." By using the motivating element of saving money, you appeal to the reader's self-interest. The self-interest makes turning down the purchase harder.

Likewise, you must know your audience. If you write about increased profits, you better write to someone who has an effect on profits. If you write for a contribution, you must know whether the individual can afford to give. Remember, when you fish, you use the bait the fish wants, not what you want.

Creating desire

We've got the reader's interest. Now let's develop desire. Stir customer desire by demonstrating all the advantages of owning the product or using the service. Tell why the product or service is important. Then paint a picture of how the product or service will benefit the reader. Here are examples:

- Improve your results with this equipment. Picture how smoothly your operations will run.
- Besides the satisfaction of giving, you'll also save on your taxes. Your contribution is tax deductible.

- Expect increased productivity with it. Watch how it will improve your performance.

Desire expands a reader's interest, so he or she wants to buy the product or act on the idea. In effect, your letter helps you develop something of value to the reader.

To show how to create that desire, let's look at home security. For attention you could start with startling statistics that show how common burglary is. For interest you talk about protection and safety. Then for desire, you suggest your product, the Bugle Burglar Alarm, as the solution and picture it as an item the reader must have to protect the home. So you might say:

> Picture the security and satisfaction the Bugle Burglar Alarm gives you and your family at night when you are sleeping. And when you take a vacation away from home, you can relax and enjoy your vacation. Let our system take the worry out of protecting your home.
>
> Here's something you should like, too: This protection is provided at an affordable price. The low installation fee depends on the type of system you want; monthly fee is only $18.50.

Generating Action

No matter how effective your appeal, you must close the deal. If readers fail to act, you fail, too. To get the results you want, never assume readers understand what action you want. Always tell them.

In business we repeatedly hear of the importance of a sense of closure. We get that sense of closure with the call to action, because it completes the effort just as finishing the dessert completes the meal.

You have one purpose with a call to action—to have readers act. That way you get the order, satisfy the complaint, or obtain the help or contribution. Here's an example of a call to action for the Bugle Burglar Alarm:

> It can happen anytime. Call us at 444-4444. Find out about the quality protection the Bugle Burglar Alarm gives and how quickly we can install it. Call today, because the sooner you call, the sooner you can have an alarm for your home that protects both you and your family.

This final paragraph tells the reader what must be done to get the alarm. Imperative sentences dot the message. "Call us . . . ," "Find out about . . . ," and "Call today . . ." state the action the reader must take. By asking for action, a seed is planted in the reader's mind. That planted seed increases the chances action will be taken.

Getting used to using imperative sentences is important, so here's another example that talks about Guaranteed Mortgage protection:

> You can't prevent a disability, but you can prevent the financial problems it may bring. Apply for Guaranteed Mortgage

```
Protection today. Just complete the enclosed application and
send it to us in the courtesy envelope. You'll be glad you
did.
```

Notice that this call to action paragraph has three imperative directives that ask for action. They are (1) "Apply for . . . ," (2) "Just complete the . . . ," and (3) "send it . . . ." With directives like this, the paragraph asks for action.

Summary of AIDA

- In the first paragraph, grab *attention*.

- Create *interest* by stating benefits, giving statistics, or answering questions.

- Develop *desire* by picturing the advantages of owning or doing what you want done.

- In the last paragraph, ask for the *action* or result you want.

Now let's look at a specific example and see how the AIDA plan works:

PERSUADING

INSURANCE AGENT ASKS HOMEOWNERS TO FIND OUT ABOUT SAFEGUARD INSURANCE

SITUATION: An insurance agent, Tom Jones, discovers a homeowner's insurance policy expires on February 14. He writes the homeowner and encourages that person to take a look at Safeguard Insurance. To accomplish this, his company supports him with a program that provides computerized analysis. Here's what he writes.

```
FIND OUT, MR. SMITH . . .

Three questions homeowners often ask about their
insurance are:

    1. Can I save money?

    2. Do I have adequate coverage for catastrophes
       like hail, tornadoes, and flooding?

    3. In case of damage, is service quick?

And those questions make sense. Each of us wants
home protection that is reasonably priced, covers
nature's disasters, and helps us recover losses
quickly. Safeguard Insurance Company does that for
you. Here are answers to those questions that show
you why:

    ANSWER 1: Yes! Safeguard Insurance can save you
```

money. Our policies are discounted substantially below the rates the state of Michigan
sets. Now isn't that a breath of fresh air?

ANSWER 2: Perhaps. Find out by taking advantage
of Safeguard's <u>free</u> computerized analysis.

ANSWER 3: You bet! With a phone call to me, you
get immediate action, personal attention, and
prompt results.

Your present homeowner's insurance policy expires
on February 14. Make a decision to take advantage
of our *free* computerized analysis, a decision that
can save you money and ensure you have adequate
protection.

Just complete and return the enclosed
questionnaire. Use the courtesy envelope and drop
it in the mail today. You'll be glad you did.

FIND OUT ABOUT YOUR HOME'S PROTECTION,

P.S. For immediate answers, pick up the phone and
call me at <u>121-1212</u>.

Analysis of the letter

- The creative substitution supplements the attention of the first paragraph and focuses the entire message.

- To capture attention three questions are asked that are of interest to homeowners. The homeowner's mind should want an answer. So we've followed the AIDA approach and created *attention*.

- This second paragraph is the *interest* paragraph. There is a feeling of agreement with the "makes sense" comment. The next sentence reaffirms the questions in the first paragraph. Then the homeowner reads that there is a solution: Safeguard Insurance.

- The answers suggest that Safeguard Insurance is the solution and plants a seed that perhaps a solution is needed. The desire is starting to take hold.

- The next paragraph uses action verbs to help paint a picture for Mr. Smith so he will find out. This supports the *desire* in the previous paragraph.

- The *action* paragraph uses imperative sentences to tell Mr. Smith what he must do.

- The creative substitution is an extension of the call to action paragraph.

- The P.S. gives Mr. Smith another way to act so he can get answers.

ANTICIPATING WHAT THE READER WANTS TO READ

Dictators tell others what to do. Authoritarians dictate orders to subordinates. And military officers give orders to privates. But people who write sales letters have to persuade.

Sales people probe and try to establish what the needs of the customer are. Then after the probe and finding out what's wanted, we try to match our product to the customer. That requires persuasion.

Unfortunately, we don't have the luxury of being able to probe when we write a letter.

We have to anticipate the reader's needs and ask, "What does that other person want?" To meet that anticipation, we have three tools to help us.

1. Using imperative sentences or those that start with *you*.

2. Avoiding the trap of features; use benefits.

3. Using descriptive adjectives to color your message.

Let's look at those tools.

Use imperative sentences or those that start with you.

We use imperative sentences to give orders and to make requests. These sentences ask people to do something: to buy, to get, to do, to open. When we persuade, we also ask others to do something. So the imperative sentence makes sense when we are persuading.

But using the imperative sentence is not enough. Today we are in a visual society. We constantly hear about how TV affects our lives. So when you have a chance to write and want to persuade, use visual power words like "Picture the results," "Imagine the opportunity," "Examine the results," "Explore the opportunities," and "Discover the improvement."

Those power words are words that can hit visual hot buttons. Take advantage of them.

Not everyone is a visual person, however. We have other senses: touch and hearing. Since the person we are writing may not be visual, sprinkle in verbs that use the other senses. For example,

- <u>Hear</u> how others have responded.
- <u>Reach out and touch</u> someone.
- <u>Feel</u> the excitement others have felt.

And we've all heard of the value of the "you" approach. Be generous with "you" when persuading. Use sentences like this:

- You find a luxury that . . .
- You'll see new ideas that . . .
- You discover a difference . . .
- You receive a benefit that . . .

Avoid the trap of features; use benefits

Just saying "you" can get you into a trap. We know "you" should exist in our correspondence. Including *you* doesn't mean, however, that we are writing an effective letter. We may be fooling ourselves. Rather than writing about what interests the reader (benefits), we may only be writing about what we think is important (features). Let me explain.

Suppose someone works for a hotel and writes this: "You'll find a terrific location."

Who cares? This comment uses *you* but only talks about a feature. The benefit comes if the location is explained. "You'll find a terrific location . . . with easy access to the airport . . . that puts you right downtown . . . that is convenient to both downtown and the airport." Those added comments tell us whether we're interested.

Similarly, someone else could write: "You'll discover we have twenty years of experience."

Again, who cares? We're only hearing a feature. What is the advantage of the experience to customers? For a benefit we'd probably want to hear language like this: "With 20 years of experience, you can expect the same quality that others have learned to rely on."

The important thing to remember when you are writing a persuading letter is not to limit yourself to what you do. Include the benefits of doing business with you. Normally the connecting words *who, that,* or *which* do the job. For example,

- You'll discover a photographer who creates memories.
- You will get the finest quality furniture, which adds elegance to your home.
- You'll experience quality that redefines what luxury means.

Use descriptive adjectives to color your message

Writing experts say to use words strong in themselves. I agree. Instead of "profits rose," write "profits skyrocketed." Instead of "profits fell," write "profits plummeted."

But, in persuading situations, we need more than words strong in themselves. We need words that hit hot buttons, that touch emotion. Descriptive adjectives are just those kind of words.

In a valid contract, there must be a meeting of the minds. When we persuade, we need a meeting of the minds, too. Descriptive adjectives help create that meeting of the minds.

For example, if I told you I was giving you information, a yawn would probably be the best I could expect from you. If I told you I was sending you valuable information, you'd probably pay more attention. The difference in my message is one word, a descriptive adjective—valuable.

Here are other examples of the descriptive adjectives:

- You'll receive <u>powerful</u> equipment that . . .
- The programs implement <u>positive</u> change . . .
- You'll discover an <u>exciting</u> adventure . . .

As you watch TV, notice how commercials inflate their messages with descriptive adjectives. How many times have you heard of new, improved such-and-such?

So the next time you write a letter and see a noun standing alone, tell yourself that you are a persuader, a seller, that you want a meeting of the minds. Then add a descriptive adjective. You'll discover you are writing a better letter.

A word of caution, however. A descriptive adjective next to every noun can be overwhelming. First, add the adjective. Then edit and determine whether the adjective strengthens the message.

ITEMS TO AVOID

When persuading, we've talked about some of the things you should do, such as using the AIDA plan and using descriptive adjectives. But there also are things we should not do when we persuade. Here are three pitfalls we should avoid:

1. Using *not*.

2. Ending with questions.

3. Exaggeration.

Now let's examine those pitfalls individually.

Using not

When you persuade, try to avoid *not*. The word *not* suggests a negative tone. Since you want a positive response, find a substitute.

AVOID	SUBSTITUTE
don't forget	remember
do not	avoid
can't give	refuse
don't like	dislike
do not approve	disapprove

These examples show other substitutions for *not*:

```
WRONG: Don't pass this up.
RIGHT: Grab it!

WRONG: Don't miss this opportunity.
RIGHT: Take this opportunity.

WRONG: You'll be sorry if you don't order now.
RIGHT: Order now.

WRONG: It doesn't start until you mail the card.
RIGHT: It starts when you mail the card.
```

On occasion *not* can be effective if you're creating a contrast or setting up a "straw man." Here's how you might use it if you are in the insurance business:

```
If you don't have Safeguard Insurance, you may be wondering if
you're paying more than you should for coverage. If that's the
case, let me make a suggestion.
```

Ending with questions

A question in the final paragraph gives the reader the option to get out, to avoid your idea or product. You make it easy to escape from your persuasion.

A question helps the reader avoid your appeal. A positive statement, however, directs your appeal. So be positive.

```
WRONG: Won't you give the XE-101 a chance? (No, why should I?)
RIGHT: Take advantage of the XE-101.

WRONG: Won't you give? (No, I gave at the office.)
RIGHT: Help us help others. Give to the United Way.

WRONG: Shouldn't you act now? (What for?)
RIGHT: Act now.

WRONG: Won't you apply today? (Why should I?)
RIGHT: Apply today.

WRONG: Will you mail the card, please, permitting me to call?
       (No. I won't.)
RIGHT: Drop the card in the mail. Let me know you'd like me
       to call.

WRONG: Let us know if you want us to do this, won't you? (Not
       on your life.)
RIGHT: Let us know you'd like us to do this. Just complete and
       return the enclosed card, and we'll do the rest.
```

Exaggeration

We've all heard people say, "I've told you a million times not to . . ." That kind of statement doesn't persuade. It's a turnoff, because it's an exaggeration.

Exaggeration takes away from the strength of our message, because if one statement is unbelievable, our mind tells us others probably are too. Then the entire message loses the reader. Moral: Avoid exaggerations that make your letter unbelievable.

Strong statements should replace exaggeration. You can do that with opinions that weaken exaggerations and language that replaces absolutes like *completely*. Here are examples:

```
WRONG: You will be completely satisfied. (No reasonable per-
       son can make this promise.)
RIGHT: I think you will be extremely satisfied. (The opinion
       weakens the exaggeration. Downgrading completely makes
       the thought believable.)

WRONG: It's the opportunity of a lifetime. (Who are we kid-
       ding?)
RIGHT: I think you'll find this a terrific opportunity. (The
       opinion couples with terrific and makes the offer sound
       real.)
```

Statements of perfection are another form of exaggeration and also need weakening; they rub people the wrong way. Words like *never* and *always* give us a warning sign. If you see them in your letters, drop them. The reader doesn't want to read language with those words. It's unsubstantiated bragging.

```
WRONG: We never make mistakes in quality. (We walk on water,
       too.)
RIGHT: You'll find superior quality in our widgets. (It's a
       strong statement, but not an absolute.)

WRONG: We always deliver on time. (Sure.)
RIGHT: Expect delivery by Thursday, January 10. (Unlike the
       first version, a definite time is provided.)
```

Checklist of "don'ts"

- Don't use *not* to persuade. Replace that negative word with something positive.

- Don't end letters with questions. End with a call to action that asks for results.

- Don't exaggerate. Make your message believable.

CHAPTER EIGHT

THE SALES PLAN, THE HOME RUN

---

*"Some of us will do our jobs well and some will not, but we
will all be judged by only one thing—the result."*
— Vince Lombardi

We want our sales letters to be like going to a baseball game. We want to see a home run.
We want results.

But getting results from sales letters is often difficult. People today are faced with an
avalanche of mail. The volume alone can overwhelm and frustrate. As a result, the circular
file probably gets more than its fair share of what we write.

With the volume of correspondence that crosses an executive's desk on an average day,
capturing attention is difficult. For instance, Malcolm Forbes once commented that he got
about 5,000 letters each year and only 10% of those were quality letters. Put another way,
that meant only 500 stood out.

What is a quality letter? How do you make your letter stand out and attract attention?
How can you be different?

In this chapter we'll discuss the sales plan; you'll learn how to write that quality sales
letter that gets noticed and stands above the crowd. You'll learn how to turn an ordinary
letter into an extraordinary sales tool.

You'll have a blueprint that will give you a jump on the competition. You'll discover
an effective approach that creates a writing difference, a difference that breaks with tradition.

Anyone can follow the crowd. But that almost guarantees a path to mediocrity. So we
won't write what everyone else writes. We'll write smarter. We'll follow the sales plan.
Here are its key elements:

1. Always use a creative substitution for the salutation.

2. Grab attention in the opening paragraph.

3. Once you have their attention, keep them interested.

4. Create desire by showing benefits.

5. Ask for action.

6. Replace the complimentary close with a creative substitution.

7. Never sign with a ballpoint pen; use a felt tip pen in a color other than black. Also, sign just your first name.

8. Use a P.S.

9. Use physical techniques to gain attention.

With the sales plan you have a consistent plan of attack. You'll get better results and free yourself for other productive work.

Now let's explore the separate aspects of the sales plan.

THE CREATIVE SUBSTITUTION

Always use creative substitutions to replace traditional salutations in any sales letter. They put pizzazz into your message.

Remember, the decision to read or not to read a sales letter is made in the first five seconds. The creative substitution expands those five seconds and increases the chances your letter will be read. The traditional salutation doesn't. It was developed only to acknowledge or identify with language like "Dear Mr. Jones," "Dear Ms. Smith," "Dear Chamber of Commerce Member," or "Dear Credit Card Holder."

In my opinion, professional writers are concerned too much with protocol and correctness. They tell us what others have done before and what is correct. They give us form and mechanics and keep us locked into tradition. They shouldn't.

In sales we want results, not form. We want customers' attention, not inattention. We want them to remember us, not forget us. And most of all, we want them to buy from us, not to leave us.

Creative substitutions don't look for correctness, they look for creativity and results. And they help us get results, because they support the sales messages in our letters.

We've all heard that being different makes a difference in sales. Creative substitutions are definitely different, because they let us break from tradition. And because of that break, they become an integral part of the sales message. They aim for results and give us that selling edge that might make the difference in making a sale.

In an earlier chapter, we discussed the creative substitution and how it works. Let's add to that discussion and include more examples. Notice that each of those that follow uses a message to set up the focus of the letter. "Dear Ms. Adams" and "Dear Mr. Thomas" could never do that.

1. A real estate company to local homeowners.
   "WE JUST SOLD 222 RIVER RIDGE!!!"

2. A printing company to a direct mail company.
   "MORE $$$ COULD BE ON THE WAY!"

3. A marketing and consulting firm to a speaker.

        `"LET US HELP YOUR SPEAKING CAREER SOAR . . ."`

4. A hotel to a meeting planner.

        `"COME AND SEE WHAT WE HAVE TO OFFER, TOM:"`

5. A tour company to a customer.

        `"CONGRATULATIONS ON CHOOSING FUN TOURS . . .`
        `. . . for your upcoming vacation."`

6. A direct mail clothing marketer to consumers.

        `"HELP! I GOOFED! WE'RE OVERSTOCKED! WE'RE HAVING A SALE!"`

7. An advertising firm to a food marketer.

        `"WHY XYZ ADVERTISING FOR YOUR COMPANY, MS. ADAMS?`
        `That's easy. Your company will have at its fingertips . . ."`

Creative substitutions jump start your sales messages so customers and clients want to continue reading. Use them to inject excitement into your message. Use them to sell.

ATTENTION—THE OPENING PARAGRAPH

The first paragraph in a sales letter is the most important. It's the paragraph that seizes customer attention and encourages others to continue reading your message. It either gets the customer's attention or loses it. If that first paragraph doesn't capture the customer's attention, the letter should never be written.

Since our writing success depends on customers wanting to read our messages, we need writing techniques to develop attention. These next writing techniques do that. They show you ideas that win customer attention.

Using an ah-ha statement

The *ah-ha* statement helps shake people out of their seats, because it startles. And something startling can only attract attention. In effect you say, "Here is an offer you can't refuse." This attention grabber then dictates further attention by readers, so they can examine more fully what sounds like something they want. They want to continue.

The *ah-ha* statement usually includes statistics, numbers, or unexpected comments. Here are examples:

- `It's frightening. In the Dallas/Fort Worth area a burglary takes place every seven minutes — a violent crime every 25 minutes. But we can fight back.`

- `Sales call expenses are escalating and today cost about $260 a call. So keeping those expenses down is important. We can't just sell. We've got to sell smart.`

Announcing the news
Customers like to hear good news first. If there is a special, a discount, or a sale, that's good news. Tell them.

- Our 50% off sale starts Thursday, August 5.
- Save $20 on your next purchase over $50. Here's how.
- It's a special travel package.

Saying "You are special"
Another approach uses the you-are-special technique. When we're told we are special, we take notice. That kind of a comment is flattering and makes us feel important. It gets our attention. Here are examples that use the you-are-special approach.

- You've earned it. Because of your excellent credit record, you've been preapproved for a credit line of $5,000.
- Your credit rating says you deserve it. So reward yourself by taking a step up to more privileges, more convenience, and more savings than ever before.
- You may be the perfect candidate for running your own business. But we're not telling you anything you don't already know.

Asking a question
Asking a question also grabs attention. These next examples use questions:

- Do you have any idea on how the investments in your portfolio will fare in the future? Should you sell? Should you stand pat?
- How do you put your sales dollars to work?
    IDENTIFYING the prospect?
        FOLLOWING UP with sales calls?
            CLOSING the sale?
- What happens to your profits in a recession? How vulnerable are you to a downturn? How can you keep market share?

Starting with a joke or story
You also can start with a joke or story. Jokes and stories suggest friendliness. And friendliness puts a smile in your letter. If the story or joke is too long or inappropriate, however, you may lose the reader—so be careful with this approach.

- There was only one thing wrong with your suggestion, Bill. I didn't think of it myself.
- His boss had just come in and wanted changes in the handouts

```
Joe had just put together. Nervous, stressed, and tired, Joe
sat wondering whether his copying equipment would give him
the performance he needed. He was worried. Would the equip-
ment handle putting a quality handout together in time for
tomorrow's meeting?
```

- ```
  When her mother died, Cindy had to grow up fast. For three
  years she had known only the comfort of a good home and the
  affection of a loving parent. Suddenly Cindy was alone.
  ```

Painting a picture

All effective writing requires the writer to paint a picture. This approach is especially important in your opening. TV advertising shows us how much fun we have when we drink a soft drink or the excitement created by owning a new convertible. But writers of sales letters never have the luxury of pictures when we write. So we have to use vivid language to suggest them.

- ```
  Picture yourself skiing on the snow-covered slopes of Vail.
  You've just started your vacation and are looking forward
  to a week of fun.
  ```

- ```
  You think of quality when you think of Cadillac or IBM. For
  value, a blue chip stock often comes to mind. You also think
  excellence when you hire an executive search firm.
  ```

- ```
  Imagine it's a few years into the future. As you're driving
  home from work, you pick up the phone and call home. Then
  you press a few buttons and turn on the heat at home. Press
  a few more and your microwave is preparing dinner for you.
  Sound farfetched?
  ```

Each of the examples leaves us hanging. Each suggests a situation that needs an answer. We have to read on.

Using quotations

Another opening technique uses quotations. You've heard them in speeches. They also work in letters. But should the quotation or the person making it be familiar? Generally yes. Only one rule should dictate the use of quotations, however—they should fit the sales message to be effective.

```
My grandfather once told me there were two kinds of people:
those who do the work and those who take the credit. He told
me to try to be in the first group; there was much less com-
petition.
                                        — Indira Gandhi
```

```
Paying attention to simple little things most men neglect
makes a few men rich.
                                        — Henry Ford
```

A man who starts out going nowhere generally gets there.
— Dale Carnegie

INTEREST

Grabbing immediate attention is only part of your effort. After the attention step, you must sell the reader on the merits of your idea or product.

One way to keep customers interested is to create a problem. Then you give a solution in that same paragraph. For instance:

```
PROBLEM: Finding a quality speaker. SOLUTION: Jay Jones. "If
you're looking for a high-energy presentation, a fun program
with new ideas, and a talk with nuts and bolts, you've got it
with my writing programs."
```

After the solution you explain why your answer is the right solution. Then add something like this that supports your solution: "Your people can expect . . ."

Another approach is to determine a need and then meet that need with what you offer. This example shows identifying the need (losing weight) and meeting it:

```
(IDENTIFYING THE NEED.) Most Americans are overweight and look
for a way to take off those extra pounds. They want to lose
weight to feel and look better. You too may want to take off
extra weight.
```

```
(MEETING THAT NEED.) You can with the PoundsOff System. It
helps you lose those pounds quickly and safely. In just a week
you look and feel better. And once you've experienced those
results, your feelings will feed on themselves. You'll want to
lose more.
```

In solving that problem or meeting that need, use words that reflect emotion; use words people respond to. Use words like *free, satisfaction,* and *success.* According to research done at Yale University, the following 12 words are the most persuasive: *discovery, easy, guarantee, health, love, money, new, proven, results, safety, save, you.*[1]

People respond differently to a sales appeal. Some will be sold with emotion. Others require logical explanations. So it's important to sprinkle both in your sales letters. Emotional language might include:

- ● Once you've experienced . . .

- ● Because it's important to you . . .

- ● Here's something we can all appreciate . . .

But emotion requires support, or logic. Many need reasons to support their emotional feelings. Statistics and supporting facts give that necessary language. Here are examples that show how you create logic or the reasons to buy:

- Another good reason you want . . .
- Examine it as a solution.
- The proposal is a sound business offer.

Creating interest means creating both emotion and logic. Here are seven techniques that help do this.

1. Advantage or benefits—emotion and logic

The most obvious approach to supporting your product, service, or idea is to tell about its advantages or benefits. You wouldn't be selling unless your item had advantages. By explaining advantages, you paint a dramatic picture of what you have that puts readers first; you let readers know that you have something they should have; and you capture their interest, so they want what you're selling.

When you explain benefits, don't focus on what a product or service is, rather focus on what it will do for your customers. Here are examples that give benefits to the customer:

- You'll find a product that will save you downtime.
- You'll be able to use the ideas immediately.
- Guaranteed for 35 years, your aluminum roof frees you around the house because it eliminates maintenance.

2. Supporting facts—logic

The advantages would also include the supporting facts like test figures and why a product or idea is good. You include these supporting items to give credibility to your message, because this information reinforces any positive thoughts the reader may have.

- <u>Road and Driver</u> picked it as the car of the year.
- Our volume allows us to make this offer.
- It received the top-quality award.

3. Guarantees—emotion and logic

Of special importance is the guarantee, something that hits customers right in the comfort zone. People like to take the hassle out of any future problems. Besides, it's comforting to know that someone else will shoulder possible breakdowns or problems.

So if your product includes a guarantee, explain its benefits to customers. Let them feel comfortable knowing that any future headaches will be handled by the company and not them.

- Our guarantee covers your car for a full five years. Any major repairs are at our expense.
- Your satisfaction is totally guaranteed. If for any reason you want to return it, we'll gladly refund your full purchase price.

- It's a lifetime guarantee. If for any reason a tool breaks, bring it to any store. You'll get a new one.

4. Testimonials—emotion

Another effective technique uses testimonials. When others read what someone else has said about the quality of your product, you suggest that same quality is available to them.

When you hear a TV ad testimonial, the testimonial suggests something good about the product. Testimonials in letters act the same way. When you have support by others about your product, you're sharing their excitement. By sharing that excitement, readers should want to grab that excitement and buy your product.

- These motivational tapes turned my life around.
- It's fun writing exciting letters. It's even more fun getting exciting results.
- You revolutionized my exercise and eating habits.

5. Free samples—emotion and logic

Providing a free sample, gift, or brochure also arouses interest, because everyone likes something free. With a free sample, customers get something without any effort. If no effort is required, then they probably will try the product. And if they try it, you have given them a reason to try it again.

- Clip the $.60 coupon to buy the sample size, or use the coupon as a discount on the full size.
- Here is the current copy of our publication.
- Try this sample widget. We think you'll like it.

6. Free trials—emotion and logic

Closely akin to the free sample is the free trial. When you have faith in your product, you want others to try it. If they try it, then you know they'll use it again. And if they use it again, you've succeeded in persuading, in selling. The trial offer gives you this opportunity to sell.

- Without cost to you, try our widget for a month.
- With your approval we'll send the next issue free.
- Use our facilities for a week, <u>free</u>.

7. Acceptance by others—emotion and logic

You may want to show how other users have accepted your product or service. By mentioning other users, you equate your item with quality. You say that if others use it, readers should, too. You're suggesting they follow the leader.

For instance, if you say that large companies use your product or idea, you suggest that using the item makes customers similar to the large companies. The implication is you're a winner just like the large companies are if you use the product.

- Over 100,000 people have used our motivation tapes. The feedback has been spectacular.

- If you want to know how we'll handle your business insurance, ask some of our clients how we handle theirs. You'll like what you hear.

- Other Fortune 500 companies have used our services. Like them, you'll receive the quality services they demand.

DESIRE

You've gotten attention. You've developed interest. Now you want readers to want your product, service, or idea. You create that desire by involving them personally in what you are selling. In effect, you couple them with the product.

How do you do this? You paint a picture that shows the customer using the product. And to paint that picture, use verbs tied to the senses. So include words and phrases like these:

TASTING: taste, experience the flavor, savor, take a bite.

SEEING: imagine, picture, examine, see.

HEARING: hear, listen, let your ears.

SMELLING: smell, sniff, put your nose.

TOUCHING: reach out, touch, feel, sense, experience.

Armed with these words, paint a picture for your customers that uses the persuasion of the senses. Then you'd have examples like these:

- Taste the excitement of . . .
- Imagine how lead time is reduced with the _____ and how it takes away production headaches.
- If you had heard the comments our customers made about the fun time they had, you'd want to share their excitement.
- You can smell the aroma of success.
- Feel the thrill of shooting the rapids . . .

THE CALL TO ACTION

Never presume the prospective customer will act just because you wrote a persuasive letter. No matter how persuasive your letter might be, always ask the customer for the order or the action you want. A persuading letter is useless when the customer fails to act on your offer.

We've all heard the comment, "If you want something, ask for it." That's exactly what the call-to-action paragraph does. It asks for it.

A topic sentence always starts your call-to-action paragraph. That topic sentence is a call-to-action sentence. For instance, when you ask for the order, time, a phone call, or action you want, start your paragraph with the result you expect to achieve. This sentence highlights your message and, in effect, provides a summary. Here are examples:

- Take advantage of this lowered price and put yourself in the luxury of a Widget automobile.

- Act now and protect one of your most valuable assets — your income.

- Join me in giving to the United Way.

Notice that each of those examples uses imperative sentences with an implied you. By using the imperative, you employ language that works like an order, that plants an idea to follow your request.

So always use the imperative for the call-to-action sentence. Without an imperative sentence, the start of the paragraph is weakened. Here are examples that show what I mean:

```
WRONG: I hope you will join the association.
RIGHT: Join the association and jump start your career.

WRONG: Won't you add the software to the package?
RIGHT: Add the software to your package.

WRONG: Please consider using our hotel for your next conven-
       tion.
RIGHT: Give your people the quality they expect in a conven-
       tion hotel.

WRONG: Thank you in advance for looking at what we have to
       offer.
RIGHT: Expect results from . . .
```

After the call-to-action sentence, you give your readers the how to's. Tell readers what they must do to get the item you talked about. And continue with imperative sentences. You want readers to act. So you use language like this:

- <u>Act</u> now to get the information. Just <u>complete</u> the enclosed card and <u>drop</u> it in mail.

- <u>Find</u> out today how the computer can help you. Just <u>visit</u> your participating authorized dealer and <u>discover</u> for yourself its features and time-saving benefits.

- <u>Examine</u> the information. Then <u>tell</u> yourself, "I like what I see." I'll call you Thursday, February 2, to see how we might work together.

In the call-to-action paragraph, *you must make response easy*. Readers may not buy or act as you want them to if you make the buying effort tedious or difficult. Make the action easy. Include items or information readers need to act.

First, *look at physical requirements* that help readers respond. Include items like order forms, telephone numbers, and courtesy envelopes. (I always call postage-paid, self-addressed envelopes, "courtesy envelopes." The tone is better, and you make the message easier to read by using only two words, not five.)

Items for ease of payment include toll-free telephone numbers, use of credit cards, postponing payment, or easy payments.

Now let's put easy response and easy payment together:

```
Put your completed order in the courtesy envelope and pay by
credit card. For an immediate response, call us at 1-800-111-
1111.
```

The last sentence in your call to action paragraph should aim for the human touch and confirm why the idea, product, or service should be used. That language generally includes a pronoun like *you, we,* or *I*. For example,

```
Find out for yourself. Call for your free rate quotation now,
while you're thinking about it. You have nothing to lose . . .
but perhaps a lot to save.
```

• • •

```
Discover the savings. Examine the enclosed price circular and
compare its prices with those you are already paying. Then
call us at 111-1111 and say, "I want to do business with you."
You'll be glad you made that call.
```

• • •

```
Come in and browse. Then take advantage of the bargains
throughout the store. You'll like what you see. I guarantee
it.
```

The five items essential to the call-to-action paragraph are:

1. First sentence—call-to-action sentence.

2. How to's.

3. Easy response.

4. Easy payment.

5. The last sentence—the human touch.

To give you a feel for these items, here are three examples with illustrative notes:

```
Experience the beauty of a well-maintained lawn (call to ac-
tion). For your free, no-obligation estimate, call (how to) us
at 111-1111 (easy response) today. We'll be right out (human
interest).
```

•   •   •

```
Enjoy the easy listening of this music offer (call to action).
Put (how to) your order in the courtesy envelope (easy
response). Then drop (action) it in the mail today. We'll bill
you later (easy payment and human interest).
```

•   •   •

```
Let the dynamics of full color help sell you (call to action).
Discover (how to) fresh marketing ideas that will enhance your
professional image. Call (action) me at 1-800-111-1111 (easy
response). You'll be glad you did (human interest).
```

THE CREATIVE SUBSTITUTION

We've finished the letter and now must have a complimentary close. If we follow tradition, then we end with "Sincerely," "Yours truly," " Best regards," or other similar, boring language.

For goodwill you substitute this kind of language:

- **HAVE A TERRIFIC DAY!!!**
- **KEEP SMILING . . .**
- **HAPPY THANKSGIVING,**

To add a persuasive message at the end, use language like this:

- **ACT NOW . . .**
- **THINK QUALITY! THINK (the name of your firm)!**
- **LET'S PUT SOMETHING TOGETHER FOR YOUR PEOPLE . . .**

Each of these creative substitutions suggests that the reader do something. So what this message does is supplement the call-to-action paragraph. Breaking tradition, we support what we asked for earlier. Rather than ending with passive tradition, we write the way we talk and end with the strength of a selling message.

Signature

Most of us never think about how we sign our letters. We should.

Do not sign with a ballpoint pen. Instead, use a felt-tip pen or a fountain pen. Why? Because the ballpoint pen is pedestrian. Everyone uses it. To be different, forget the ballpoint.

Next, sign in a color other than black. Black is an authoritarian color. It suggests power. When you're selling, you don't want to deal from a power position. That can be intimidating.

So what do you use? Anything other than black. My preference is either blue or red.

If you are in front of a large audience and ask, "What is your favorite color," the answers will be overwhelmingly blue and red. Blue is the trusting color so it is always appropriate. Red is the attention color.

I use a red, felt-tip pen to sign all my letters. Besides getting attention, red also matches my letterhead. If you have a letterhead with a color, you should probably use the same color for your signature.

And when you sign your name, sign only your first name. By signing your first name, you've given the other person license to call you by your first name. That means you have an implied license to call that person by his or her first name.

When you're on a first-name basis, rapport and friendship set in. When you have friendship, resistance comes down. When resistance comes down, it's easier to get cooperation and a sale. So use the first name.

Unless you have your own letterhead, type your name and title under the signature to identify yourself.

Postscript or P.S.

The P.S. works. Always use it in sales letters.

Here's why. When we receive a letter, our eyes look for what might be interesting. The salutation (creative substitution) and first paragraph do that. But so does the P.S. In fact, studies show that often the P.S. is the first part of the letter that is read.[2] If that's the case, we better take advantage of its pulling power.

And if it's not read first, it surely will be read last.[3] Either way we win if we have a powerful message in it.

Here's what pros say about the P.S.:

> Time and again, a postscript has proven effective in increasing orders . . . . The P.S. is one of the most read parts of any direct mail letter. Most people read the postscript before they read the letter.[4]

> Many of the model letters have a *postscript*. This is not an afterthought, but a planned part of the letter. The reason for using the *postscript* is to attract attention. This is accomplished by placing the added remarks outside of the letter and at the end, where emphasis is strongest. Just how much emphasis is added is a matter of choice. Some writers of sales letters use it consistently and some not at all, but it does add a little punch to the end of the letter.[5]

> Test after test has seemed to prove that letters mailed with a P.S. will out-pull those mailed without one.[6]

These comments show that the P.S. works. And if it works, you should use it.

PHYSICAL TECHNIQUES

Physical techniques help you gain attention and catch the customer's eye. Knowing these techniques can make a difference in your results.

Before discussing them, however, recognize that there is a difference between a sales letter to an individual or a small group and direct mail to a mass audience. Normally, both use the same approach. When we're talking mass mailings, however, we're talking direct mail, and we do have exceptions with it.

For instance, in direct mail you can have the luxury of a second color in the body of the letter, because volume keeps the cost of color down. Also, direct mail uses long letters with good results. We'll discuss these differences as we go through this section.

Letterhead paper

Studies show that 73.2% of all mail is delivered in white envelopes[7] and that suggests white stationery. So if you want to be like everyone else, use white. Because industry uses white so extensively, however, I recommend a letterhead on colored paper with a matching envelope.

When there is a choice between a white or colored envelope or letterhead, readers will generally pick the colored one. That's a slight edge all of us should want.

While the most effective color is ivory,[8] other colors are effective, too. For instance, an ocean resort might use a pale blue to reflect a refreshing ocean, a hotel in the mountains might use light green to capture lush green forests or a challenging golf course, and a financial institution could use a gray to convey its conservative style.

For direct mail pieces with a special promotion, companies sometimes use hot pink or other bright colors to help make the message jump off the paper. Do not, however, use hot pink or shocking colors for a letterhead. Those colors can be offensive for ordinary correspondence.

A second color

Except for direct mail, a second color in the body of the letter is generally impractical for reasons of cost. But second colors for the logo or design of the letterhead make sense. When you order letterhead, you order in large quantities, and that volume reduces the cost for color in your letterhead.

In direct mail, marketers often use a second color to highlight benefits or important selling points. There the cost of color is reasonable because of the large volumes of letters used. Blue is the most common color, because it allows you to sign in blue ink, the standard color for signing letters.[9] Red, however, is probably the most powerful color for drawing attention to the reader.

Visual aids from type

Sales letters consistently take advantage of visual techniques we get from the typewriter, word processor, or printer. These include underlined words, CAPITAL LETTERS, dashes— - - - , bullets • •, dots . . ., exclamation points !!!, and
> paragraphing that gives
> > an appearance of
> > > being different.

These visual techniques help the eye pick up important items in the letter. They make reading easier. And if you make the reading easier, you're helping customers remember the message.

Type variety
With today's modern typewriters, word processors, and printers, different fonts and type styles are available at a push of a button. Those styles are nice, but stick with tradition in a sales letter.

The human mind accepts the traditional style. Variations give an excuse to reject the message. For instance, a letter with script, just because of its difference, makes reading harder. That lessens the odds your message will be read. Conclusion: stay with traditional type style.

There are two type varieties we should use, but only sparingly and only for emphasis. These are *italics* and **bold** lettering. These variations highlight important thoughts or messages and help readers both pick up and remember key words or phrases.

When using italics, use it only to make words, sentences, or quotations stand out. The eye notices variations. If the variation becomes overwhelming, however, we'll probably lose the reader. When we're selling, we can't afford a lost customer.

Bold lettering is the other type variation I recommend. Use it to highlight specific benefits or points. And to create an effective, eye-appealing letter, always use bold lettering for the creative substitutions.

Headlining between paragraphs
To grab attention and help customers' eyes follow and remember items in the letter, direct mail experts often use headlining between paragraphs. They generally CAPITALIZE ALL THE LETTERS IN THE MESSAGE, Underline Each Word Separately and Capitalize the First Letter of Each Word, or Underline the entire message and capitalize just the first letter of the first word.

In addition, these pros center the headline so the reader or customer sees a definite change in thought. Here are three examples:

TAKE ADVANTAGE OF IT—

MAIL YOUR ENROLLMENT APPLICATION TODAY.

• • •

You Must Be 100% Satisfied—

Or Your Money Back!

• • •

When you start at the top,

it's easier to work your way to the top.

Handwriting

Handwritten notes in a letter shout for attention. Whenever you use them, you're guaranteed they will be read. They personalize your message, because they stand out. And their location can be anywhere in margins, at the end of a letter, or even at the beginning.

Sentence length

In sales letters, always write short, snappy sentences. They'll help keep your reader interested.

While there is no correct length for a sentence, there is an average length that works. For a sales letter I recommend an average length of 10 words.

Why? A long sentence requires extra concentration to understand the message. If extra concentration is needed, we can expect to lose many readers. In a selling letter, we never want to lose any readers. We want them to look at the entire message, to increase our chances of getting the sale.

To help me with my sentence length, I've devised my own guideline. Whenever my computer has over two lines of typed copy in a sentence, that's a red flag. I know the sentence is too long and must be shortened. Try it!

Paragraph length

The key is letting the reader know that the letter is manageable. First impressions and appearance pay dividends. That means we must use white space to break up paragraphs. My suggestion to give that appearance: limit your paragraphs to five lines.

A good example of appearance is the 1040 tax form. The government is tricky here. They keep their paragraphs short and out initial impression is that the form will be easy to read and understand. No such luck!

But the 1040 tax form gives us a clue. Appearance gives an impression. Take advantage of appearance to give your letter an impression that it will be easy to read.

What about one-sentence paragraphs? To create emphasis, a one-sentence paragraph is often just what you want. For instance, if your first paragraph started with a one-sentence question, readers would want to read on. Here's an example: "Have you ever wanted a promotion?"

Letter length

With any letter you might ask, "Is it too long, too short, or just right? How will readers react? What is the proper length?

Abraham Lincoln was asked how long a man's legs should be. He answered, "Long enough to touch the ground."

Like leg length, there is no correct answer about letter length. Each letter must stand on its own. And because each letter stands on its own, many opinions exist on length. My recommendation: generally keep your letters to one page and no longer than a page and a half. Here's why.

Lengthy sales letters overwhelm. The wastebasket seems the only proper place for them. When I receive a long sales letter, I'm ready to give up. I rarely have the time to plow through a long dissertation. My reaction should be a tip-off to those professional writers who weigh us down with their well-prepared prose. Length turns us off.

If we feel frustrated about a long sales letter as readers, how can we write a long sales letter and hope to eliminate frustration? Can we burden readers with length and expect them to become customers and buy? I don't think so.

About four years ago I received an eleven-page letter that offered me a free seminar if I paid my expenses to get there. The first paragraph asked me to give 15 minutes of my time to discover a wonderful opportunity.

Because of the length, I didn't read the letter and didn't discover what the wonderful opportunity was. I knew the letter would be tedious reading and immediately began asking, "Why do I have to read so much? Why must I plow through all this?"

Seeing that long letter, I immediately questioned the value of the message and any possible benefits. In effect, the length put me on the defensive. I didn't *want* to be interested.

Think about length. Writing's purpose is to make readers comfortable; length only attacks comfort and takes readers out of their comfort zone.

So keep your letters short. Try to limit them to one page. With all the demands we have on our time today, a concise and short letter can be like a breath of fresh air.

If, however, you feel you need to include more information, do. But do it with attachments and enclosures.

There is an exception to short letters—direct mail. Often seminars or other items are described on an 11" by 17" page folded to give four pages. Those letters provide effective mass mailing. In addition, many magazines use lengthy letters to sell subscriptions and have found the longer letter to be effective.

Here's what one direct mail authority wrote:

> Write as much copy as you need to tell your story. No more, no less. But note:
> A two-page letter tends to pull better than a one-page letter, and a four-page
> letter tends to pull better than a two-page letter.[10]

Dates and inside address

Most correspondence requires an inside address and a date. In direct mail, however, both are often omitted.

Screening

Screening gives an added visual effect. It's a technique that gives the appearance of an added color even though another color isn't used. For instance, black can be screened to make it look gray. An example follows this paragraph.

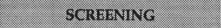

The prescript

The prescript is used in mass mailing. It's a headline that comes before the body of a letter and gives focus to the letter's content. It normally replaces the creative substitution. These beginning comments are designed to hook the reader and grab attention.

The prescript acts like the first sentence of a sales letter; it attracts attention. And because the prescript makes sense, the direct mail people already use the prescript for their mass mailings.

Not only do the direct mail people use the headline or prescript, they also use what is called the Johnson's Box, "a box at the top of many direct mail letters that is made up of asterisks. It contains one or two sentences that serve the purpose of a headline or lead."[11] Here's an example:

```
*************************************************

    A $30.00 value, yours for just $2.

      The Tax Guide for America's

    leading professional tax advisors.

*************************************************
```

A Johnson's Box can also use solid lines rather than asterisks. Or it can have no border and just be a block of copy.[12]

The direct mail people use the prescript to develop their persuasive messages. In it they make statements that give benefits, make suggestions, and offer startling comments. Here are examples:

```
*************************************************

AFFORDABLE HEALTH INSURANCE IS RIGHT AT YOUR FINGERTIPS!

*************************************************
```

```
*************************************************

     As someone

          familiar with . . .

               Creative Training Techniques

*************************************************
```

```
*************************************************

          WIN LARGER FEES

*************************************************
```

Summary of physical techniques
Remember, physical techniques help make that good impression, catch the reader's eye,

and capture attention. They dramatically increase the odds that the reader will read and remember your message.

How do you use these physical techniques? How do you take advantage of them? How can you see what works? Copy the experts. Just check the promotional mail you receive at home and learn from what you see. Discard what turns you off and borrow ideas you like. By doing this, you're taking advantage of the best creative minds in the industry!

SUMMARY—THE SALES PLAN

Knowing how to craft a sales letter puts you a step above your competition. Put the ideas you just learned to work for you; you'll see improved results in your work. Here is an outline form of the sales plan.

1. The creative substitution—always use it in the salutation.

2. Attention—the opening paragraph—use techniques that grab attention.

   - Use an *ah-ha* statement.
   - Announce the news.
   - Say "You are special."
   - Ask a question.
   - Start with a joke or story.
   - Paint a picture.
   - Use quotations.

3. Interest—use approaches that couple emotion with logic.

   - List advantages or benefits.
   - Give supporting facts.
   - Give guarantees.
   - Use testimonials.
   - Enclose free samples.
   - Use free trials.
   - Tell of acceptance by others.

4. Desire—show the product's or idea's advantages with words that use the five senses.

   - Tasting: taste, experience the flavor, savor, take a bite.
   - Seeing: imagine, picture, examine, see.
   - Hearing: hear, listen, let your ears.
   - Smelling: smell, sniff, put your nose.
   - Touching: reach out, touch, feel, sense, experience.

5. The call to action—always ask for what you want.
   - In the first sentence of the final paragraph, use a call-to-action phrase.
   - Use imperative sentences to ask for action.
   - Provide a "how to."
   - Make response and payment easy.
   - Add a human interest sentence for the last sentence.

6. The creative substitution—always use it in the complimentary close.

7. The signature.
   - Use a felt tip or fountain pen.
   - Use a colored signature.
   - Sign only your first name.

8. Postscript or P.S.—it improves response in a sales letter.

9. Physical techniques—they help the eye want to read the letter.
   - Letterhead paper.
   - A second color.
   - Visual aids from the typewriter.
   - Type variety.
   - Headlining between paragraphs.
   - Handwriting.
   - Sentence length.
   - Paragraph length.
   - Letter length.
   - Dates and inside address.
   - Screening.
   - The prescript.

The five examples we'll discuss include:

1. Asking customers to acquire a line of credit.
2. Asking for a courtesy card response.
3. Asking for calls from potential clients.
4. Welcoming a new employee.
5. Encouraging new Chamber of Commerce members to become active in the Chamber.

ASKING CUSTOMERS TO ACQUIRE A LINE OF CREDIT

SITUATION: XYZ Bank has started a new program, PREFERRED PLUS, which allows customers to have a line of credit that lets them borrow without red tape. Here's the letter asking customers to use the new program.

TAKE ADVANTAGE OF IT, MR. SMITH:

Preferred customers like you can now have a personal line of credit from $5,000 to $100,000 by just writing a check. With our new service, PREFERRED PLUS, your approved credit line is at your fingertips.

You never have to plow through any loan approval. You've already been approved. Just write a check and the money is yours.

XYZ Bank is introducing this new service, PREFERRED PLUS, for our select customers. With this new service, you can now borrow money any time you want. That means you can immediately take advantage of opportunities as they occur.

An exciting vacation in Hawaii. You've got it. An unexpected trip to Europe. You've got it. Or a new car. You've got it. PREFERRED PLUS is there for you.

Give yourself the luxury of an approved line of credit tied to the *Wall Street Journal*'s prime rate. Yes, act now and take advantage of PREFERRED PLUS. Just complete the enclosed application and send it to us in the courtesy envelope today. We'll do the rest.

GIVE YOURSELF A BONUS!!!

President

P.S. Now you can apply for PREFERRED PLUS in the comfort of your own home or office. Call 1-800-111-1111. We'll take your application over the phone and call you back with an answer.

Analysis of the letter

- Creative substitution asks for action.
- An *ah-ha* sentence starts the letter.
- Now the bank explains the new program and how easy it is to use and take advantage of.
- Desire is created by painting a picture of Hawaii, Europe, and a new car, and saying "You can have it."
- The call-to-action paragraph uses three persuading techniques: call to action, how-to for easy response, and human interest.
- The complimentary close strengthens the entire letter. "Sincerely" just doesn't seem to fit.
- The P.S. makes taking action easy.

ASKING FOR A COURTESY CARD RESPONSE

SITUATION: The Weight-Loss Company wants to include a diet program in chiropractor offices. The results depend on getting the attention of chiropractors and getting them to call. The letter is the door opener.

WATCH YOUR PRACTICE GROW, DR. JONES:

You'll discover a unique service that increases patient traffic, adds income, and blends easily into your regular practice. You'll help patients continue under your care by having them help themselves. You'll have a winner.

As a chiropractor, your special training uniquely qualifies you to treat the neuro-muscular-skeletal system. You, more than any other kind of doctor, know how important overweight problems are to that system. And helping you help your patients' weight problems is where we come in.

We are introducing a safe, effective weight-loss program available only to chiropractors. This new WEIGHT-LOSS Program effectively compliments your regular practice. We know you have questions. Let me address them.

"Will it make me money?" Yes. You have a highly researched, professional health-care program that can create a powerful profit center for you. We show you how to generate those profits.

"Will it help my patients?" Definitely yes. Weight is one of the major factors causing imbalance in body structure. WEIGHT-LOSS helps you help your overweight patients win their weight battle.

"Where will I get the time?" Your staff, not you, shows overweight patients how to help themselves with WEIGHT-LOSS. You supervise. Your staff administers. And to keep your staff's time productive, we provide them with on-site training.

"Is it covered by insurance?" We've had excellent success with workmen's compensation. And some insurance companies also pick up the tab when weight loss is prescribed by the doctor as part of a health program.

Find out what a WEIGHT-LOSS Program offers you and how WEIGHT-LOSS creates FREE word-of-mouth advertising for your office. For more information, invest a few minutes to complete and return the enclosed courtesy card. You'll be glad you did.

WEIGH THE BENEFITS!!!

P.S. To get more information immediately, pick up the phone and call me today at 1-800-111-1111. The sooner we get in touch, the sooner you can use WEIGHT-LOSS to increase patient traffic.

Analysis of the letter

- The creative substitution uses a sales message.
- The first paragraph announces good news immediately to get attention.
- The second paragraph uses the you-are-special approach, creates a need, and then meets that need.
- For added attention, the letter says the program is safe and there will be questions.
- The next four paragraphs create interest with questions. Then, with the answers, desire is generated.
- The call-to-action paragraph uses a number of action steps. They include a call to action, imperative sentence, ease of response, and human interest.
- The creative substitution strengthens the message.
- The P.S. gives another easy response and adds human interest.

ASKING FOR CALLS FROM POTENTIAL CLIENTS

SITUATION: Refund Services wants to help large utility users check their utility bills and see if they are entitled to refunds. The company is writing each of the hotels in the area and asking them to call.

THE UTILITY COMPANIES MAY OWE YOUR BUSINESS . . .

. . . CASH REFUNDS!!!

WE AVERAGE ONE OR MORE REFUNDS FOR 93% OF OUR CLIENTS

(Inside Address)

Interested? Here are recent results for those who were interested.

1. $100,000 (large fast-food chain)
2. $35,000 (hotel from large chain)
3. $29,000 (hotel from large chain)

These results show it's worth your while to investigate whether you've been overcharged. That's where we come in.

Our experience shows you may be billed more for electric, gas, and water utilities than you should be. Through a careful analysis of prior bills, we determine whether you've been overcharged and are entitled to a refund. When you are, we take the necessary steps to recover those overcharges.

At no expense to you, we make the investigation. Only when a refund is recovered does our 50% fee go into effect. We do not, however, participate in future savings resulting from this service. These are yours.

Take advantage of the service of REFUND SERVICES and discover how we can help you. For further information, just drop the completed reply card in the mail or call me at 1-800-111-1111. You'll be glad you did.

ANTICIPATE RESULTS . . .

Vice President, Marketing

P.S. Discover how REFUND SERVICES can save you money. The sooner you contact us, the sooner we can start to work for you.

Analysis of the letter

- Create a problem in the salutation.
- State results.
- Create interest by including others.
- Provide *ah-ha* statistics.

- Reinforce the statistics.
- Give a solution to the problem.
- Create desire with free service and customer benefits.
- The call to action uses imperative sentences and ease of response.
- Complimentary close reinforces the call to action with a command.
- A P.S. is a must in a sales letter.

WELCOMING A NEW EMPLOYEE

SITUATION: XYZ Corporation has just hired Tom Smith as a plant manager for one of its major operations. The letter reinforces the decision Tom made to join XYZ. The president of the company is writing because Tom is a key addition to the operation. The president resells Tom on joining the company.

YOU'LL LIKE YOUR DECISION, TOM . . .

You should fit right in. Your experience suggests you'll have everything under control after just a short time on the job.

Your employment begins Monday, March 1. I know you're looking forward to joining us. We're looking forward to having you. Welcome aboard.

As your days on the job pass, you'll find rewarding challenges to make your job exciting. I know I did when I had your job.

You've taken on a major responsibility. I can't wait to say, "Keep up the good work."

LET'S MAKE 1992 A GREAT ONE!!!

P.S. Let me know if you need anything. We'll get right on it.

Analysis of the letter

- The creative substitution uses a friendly message to get the letter started on a strong note.

- The attention paragraph uses you-are-special language.

- The interest paragraph talks of the need to belong and meets that need.

- The desire paragraph has the key word *find*.

- The call to action is more human interest than anything. But it uses "Keep up . . ."

- The creative substitution asks for good work.

- The P.S. lets Tom know he'll get help whenever he needs it.

ENCOURAGING NEW CHAMBER OF COMMERCE MEMBERS TO BECOME ACTIVE IN THE CHAMBER

SITUATION: The _____ Chamber of Commerce sends a welcoming letter to all new members of the Chamber. The letter does more than welcome, however. In addition, it resells the merits of the Chamber and encourages participation in Chamber activities.

WELCOME, MS. _____:

As a new _____ CHAMBER member, you'll discover a wealth of benefits that the _____ CHAMBER OF COMMERCE offers. Take advantage of them.

As Chairman of the Board, I know the benefits are there. I also know participation in CHAMBER activities will expose you to those benefits sooner. So become involved. By being active, you'll accelerate your knowledge of how the CHAMBER can help you.

Just as you seek "win-win" situations for your business, you'll find that active CHAMBER participation is also a "win-win" situation. You'll meet valuable contacts, be exposed to new ideas, and help shape the direction of the CHAMBER.

So get active and discover how your CHAMBER investment helps you and your company. And remember, the sooner you get involved, the sooner you'll reap the benefits of _____ CHAMBER membership.

ENJOY THE CHAMBER . . .

CEO

P.S. Be sure to attend the "_____ After Hours Business Card Exchange" on May 1st at the Essex Hotel. It's a great way to make valuable contacts.

P.P.S. To help your involvement get started, we've enclosed a list of CHAMBER activities for May.

Analysis of the letter

- A friendly creative substitution starts the letter.
- Attention comes with "wealth of benefits" and the directive of "Take advantage."
- The desire step talks of benefits that "help you."
- The interest step lists specifics to get win-win benefits.
- The call to action uses two imperatives, *get* and *discover*.
- "Sincerely" bites the dust again.
- Both postcripts support the message, "get involved."

CHAPTER NINE

HOW TO COMPLAIN AND GET RESULTS

Discover how to get results by first suggesting a solution.

"You're a crook."

"You fouled up."

"Drop dead."

These words might express just how you feel when a firm botches up an order or substitutes lesser quality products. Yes, you're angry. But avoid these expressions when writing a complaint letter. Anger rarely pays dividends.

Everyone has heard of Murphy's Law: "If something can go wrong, it will." Businesses make mistakes, too.

Most businessmen are honest and want to do what is right. To stay in business, the customer must be serviced. Consequences for failure to perform could include lawsuits, bad publicity, reduced profits, or losses.

Because of potential consequences, most businesses treat consumer complaints seriously. For instance, complaints could negatively affect the firm's image. Dissatisfaction could reduce sales. Or complaints might suggest long-range problems—like the manufacture of poor quality goods—that the company must act on.

Before beginning a complaint letter, put yourself in the proper frame of mind. Think positively. Start with the assumption you will be satisfied, that corrective action will be taken. Assume your problem, while serious to you, may help the company you're writing do a better job. With this attitude, your anger should evaporate, and you can get to the business at hand—complaining.

Yet, to get results, you need a plan when you complain. Without a plan there is no direction, so getting favorable results is probably a hit-or-miss proposition. To overcome any lack of direction, I suggest the complaint plan incorporating these eight steps:

1. Always use the creative substitution for the salutation to get attention.

2. In the first sentences of the first paragraph, create added attention by reinforcing the creative substitution.

3. State your solution, not the problem, as the last sentence of the first paragraph.

4. Explain the problem history.

5. Justify the solution.

6. Ask for the solution as the last sentence of the letter.

7. Omit the complimentary close.

8. Consider a postscript and carbon copy only as a last resort.

Here is an example of a complaint letter that follows the complaint plan.

COMPLAINT
PLAN

```
First Bankcard Center          SUBJECT:
account # 000000

Anywhere, U.S.A.

COMPUTERS MAKE MISTAKES:

Your computer must have been on a coffee break.
Your computer-generated statement charged too much.
Credit my company's account for $660.12.

Some computer error must have occurred in the
company's account. The bill showed a billing for
airplane tickets to Miami, Florida. Yet our company
does no business in Florida and never has. In fact,
we conduct business only on the West Coast. These
tickets should never have been charged to our
account.

Even if a convention had been in Miami, our people
would not have gone. Company policy requires that
employees fly only in a radius of 1,000 miles from
company headquarters. There are no exceptions.

The invoice indicates this charge:

   9-6 19123439478432833      Corrupt Airlines

                              Nowhere, U.S.A. $660.12

To help you, I've enclosed a copy of the bill with
the error marked in yellow.

You've handled our billing beautifully in the past.
Handle it beautifully again. Yes, review the bill.
```

```
Then credit the account for $660.12.

Joe Watchfulleye
Account Manager
```

We've looked at an example of a complaint letter that uses the complaint plan. Now let's investigate the parts and see how using the complaint plan affects the development of a complaint letter.

Creative substitution

Always start a complaint letter with a creative substitution to capture reader attention. As you write complaint letters, you will create many ideas to capture the attention of the reader. I know I have, and it's been fun thinking them up. Rather than letting my anger build over the complaint, I set out to get my creative juices flowing. I want to be clever. And here's a few I have used:

- SOMEBODY GOOFED:

- IT DOESN'T ADD UP:

- FIRST PRIZE? NO. LAST? PERHAPS.

- WHY?

- WHEN?

In addition to those, there is one that will always stand out in my mind. I had received a letter that offered me a free issue of a magazine if I signed and returned a card that was enclosed with the letter. If I asked for the first issue, an invoice would come with it. I signed and returned the card.

Then both the magazine and invoice arrived. Now I had two choices. I could pay for the subscription and continue receiving the magazine. Or, I could write cancel on the invoice and return it to the magazine. Then no additional magazines would be sent.

After examining the magazine, I decided it was not for me and returned the invoice with cancel written on it. A month later, I received another issue and another invoice. I also returned my second invoice with cancel on it.

Then I received a collection letter asking me to pay for the magazine subscription. That letter didn't make me a happy camper. Rather, it upset me. What really got me was how the letter started. It said:

```
Dear Mr. Jones:

Frankly, I'm at a bit of a loss. A number of weeks ago you
ordered _____ and asked us to bill you.
```

They wanted money from me for a magazine subscription I had cancelled. Was I ever angry. But I let my pen calm my anger. I started thinking how I might answer. Here's what I came up with:

FRANKLY, I'M AT A BIT OF A LOSS:

```
I kept my part of the bargain, reviewing my free
copy of _____ and deciding whether or not your
magazine was for me. It wasn't. The invoices
(copies enclosed) you've been sending aren't,
either.

Please correct your records.

Jay Jones
```

I echoed their distasteful words, and I know I got their attention. The magazine and invoices stopped coming. I had let my creativity replace my anger. My focus was on writing the letter, not my anger toward the magazine.

That magazine problem seemed sticky to me. But what about situations where we are confident we'll get immediate satisfaction? Do we write the same way? No, we don't.

Some situations may suggest an easy solution because of an obvious mistake. In that case I recommend a friendly creative substitution that says

I NEED YOUR HELP:

This creative substitution catches attention and suggests friendliness rather than a possible conflict. Most of us when asked to help, do. We're just asking for help here. The company will probably help us solve our problem.

My last suggestion about using creative substitutions in complaint letters is never to use a name with them. Since our purpose is to get results, we should keep correspondence impersonal. The impersonal approach puts recipients in a position in which they can take action without having to defend themselves.

Leave the names and name calling to someone else. (Besides, many times when we are complaining, we don't know who will get our letter.)

Opening paragraph—attention
Use the first sentences to continue the attention-getting power of the creative substitution. Use those sentences to hook the reader.

You want results to follow your complaint. You can only get those results when you have the reader's attention. So use language in the first sentence or sentences to corral that attention.

This next complaint example shows the attention-getting power of the creative substitution coupled with its supporting cast, the first sentences of the first paragraph:

FROSTY THE SNOWMAN WOULD MELT:

```
That's right. He'd be so hot he'd melt. Cool off the situa-
tion.
```

What does this example mean? It means you've started your complaint with creative language that captures attention and suggests a problem. Nothing more.

By getting attention, we're on the path to getting a meeting of the minds. Our reader is going to read our letter and pay attention to what we say.

Countless variations exist of coupling of the creative substitution with the first sentences. Only your imagination limits the extent of what you can use. As you use the complaint plan more often, you'll find attention variations easier to write.

To get you started with a feel for this approach, here are three examples:

```
CREDIT IS IMPORTANT:
Sloppy credit records are not. They impeach reputations.
```

● ● ●

```
WE NEED YOUR HELP:
In the past you've given us A+ treatment. Now transfer some of
that A+ treatment to our account.
```

● ● ●

```
SOMETHING'S GOOFY:
Two plus two equals four, and that's great. But it's not great
that our premium doesn't add up.
```

Opening paragraph—the solution

Never, never state what the problem is at the start of a complaint letter. Always start with a solution. And put that solution as the last sentence of the first paragraph.

After getting attention with the creative substitution and the first sentences, immediately follow with the solution you want in the first paragraph's last sentence. With both attention and action in the first paragraph, you hook the reader and promptly let that person know what you want before your complaint can be ignored.

In the traditional approach to complaining, the problem is stated first. It shouldn't be. Human nature tells us that people rarely want to hear about problems.

How many times have you been trapped in conversation in which someone explains how miserable he is or what a devastating situation she is in? Wouldn't the problem be easier to listen to if you heard a solution or if corrective steps had been taken?

So use this same philosophy when you complain—state initially what you want: the solution. Suggest an answer, not a problem. Notice these next contrasting examples that give either problems or solutions:

```
PROBLEM: My XYZ computer broke.
SOLUTION: Either repair or replace my XYZ computer.

PROBLEM: Our china shipment arrived partially damaged.
SOLUTION: Replace the damaged china we ordered.
```

You'll find a solution gives you a powerful start to your complaint. And you can make it even stronger. Put the solution in an imperative sentence. Make your solution sound like a directive.

For emphasis, underline the solution. The underlining is a visual technique that helps the eye pick up what you're saying.

Now let's examine the previous examples we just discussed and add a solution to them.

FROSTY THE SNOWMAN WOULD MELT:

```
That's right. He'd be so hot he'd melt. Cool off the situa-
tion. Get your drivers to our loading docks on time.
```

• • •

CREDIT IS IMPORTANT:

```
Sloppy credit records are not. They impeach reputations. Clear
our credit record.
```

• • •

WE NEED YOUR HELP:

```
In the past you've given us A+ treatment. Now transfer some of
the A+ treatment to our account. Credit us for the duplicate
charge on our printing order.
```

• • •

SOMETHING'S GOOFY:

```
Two plus two equals four, and that's great. But it's not great
that our premium doesn't add up. Reduce our premium by
$3,444.21.
```

By giving a solution rather than a problem, readers are forced to read on. They need to know why you're giving a solution and whether it's justified. They're hooked.

Besides getting readers hooked, you receive another benefit by giving the solution first. A solution gives readers a point of departure, a place to start from. And with a definite solution, you plant a seed that your solution is the right solution. Then a meeting of the minds becomes easier. You are on your way to the result you want.

You may say, "Hold it. Many complaints need more than a simple solution."

You're right. For instance, you might be faced with an unexpected price increase. Use your creativity to obtain a compromise or rollback. The principles are the same. Create attention and then couple it with the solution. Here are two examples that ask for explanations:

WE WERE SPEECHLESS:

```
It flabbergasted us. The price increase put us on the carpet
and hurts. Roll back the price increase for another month to
give us time to adjust. Let us know what we must do.
```

• • •

GOOFPROOF IT:

When we make mistakes, we want to hear about them. They can hurt business. Your goof hurt our business. Correct your delivery delays and tell us what you are going to do about them.

When you feel complications might happen or more drastic action is needed, rock the boat. When you rock the boat, the reader must stop the rocking. Here's an approach that should rock the boat and stir up action:

SOMETHING STINKS:

If I ran your credit department like your company does, you'd fire me. Credit our account for $635.99.

The body—history of the problem

Before tackling the complaint, be sure you have all the data needed to support your claim. Without proper supporting information, the odds of having the complaint settled are slim.

To act on your complaint and resolve your problem, the company needs information about the problem. So give adequate details and history necessary for identification. The offending company will be unable to help unless you give the complete story. So include items like these:

- Your name, address, and telephone number.

- Your credit card number.

- The date and place the problem happened.

- The product name and model or identification number.

- Whether or not a guarantee or warranty covers the product or service.

- A copy of the invoice.

When you send information, however, never send originals. Send copies. That way if any of the information is lost or misplaced, you still have your originals and can make other copies.

Also, if you send several pieces of information, identify each one clearly. You can mark them 1, 2, 3, and so on at the top of the page. And to make the numbering stand out, use a colored pen.

This numbering gives you two benefits. First, you can easily refer to the numbered items in your letter. Second, the reader will also find the numbering easy to follow. You both win.

Now let's discuss a specific situation. Assume you buy some tools from a supplier and the tools fail to work. To get replacement tools, you must give the problem history. You might then include:

- The problem (the tools didn't work).

- The credit card number.

- The name of the tools and model number.

- The date and place of purchase.

- The date the tools failed to work.

- The price of the tools.

- An invoice.

The tool failure undermines your productivity, so explain your difficulties. Since you or your people have lived with them, you are certainly qualified to write about them.

The body—the why or problem justification

When you go to the boss, the boss never wants to hear problems from you. The boss wants to hear answers or solutions to problems. For instance, if you say corporate image needs to be improved, you only succeed in creating a problem. Instead, you need to supply answers.

For example, when you suggest advertising, corporate participation in community events, or individual participation in civic clubs, you provide answers. By providing specifics, you show that you look for solutions.

Likewise, you give solutions when you complain. But the complaint must be reasonable. Never ask for something you are not entitled to. For instance, if the gas company tears up your yard to repair a gas leak, you could ask that the damaged part of the yard be restored. But you would not ask that the entire yard be resodded. If you ask for resodding of the entire yard, why not ask for a sprinkler system, too?

When your complaint request is reasonable, the reader can pay attention to you. You have, in effect, made action possible, since you've suggested what should be done to make things right.

Persuasion plays an important role here. Solutions are fine, but you had better tell why. You must justify your position. Your justification then gives readers a place to hang their hats. And if you give readers a place to start from, you should have the meeting of the minds you want.

Let's look at a situation in which you ask for water damage expenses to your luggage after a flight. A heavy rainstorm occurred while your luggage was being removed from your plane and taken to baggage claim. You've incurred cleaning expenses and damaged shoes.

COMPLAINT PLAN

```
Andy Airlines
Baggage Service
Box XXXX
Houston, TX XXXXX

I NEED YOUR HELP:

Flying to Houston with you was enjoyable. The
damage to my luggage, however, was not enjoyable.
Reimburse me for $95.13.
```

When I flew into Houston from Ft. Lauderdale,
Houston was experiencing heavy rains. As I looked
out the window, I noticed your people were prepared
for the weather. They were covered up. And they
should have been.

Customer luggage was not so lucky, however. My
cloth suitcase was drenched and the contents
soaked. Apparently, no preparation was made for
protecting the luggage from the elements. Ouch! I
experienced rain damage to the contents of my
luggage.

Leaving the airport, I noticed my luggage was wet
but didn't pay much attention to it. When I got
home, I discovered the damage the water had done.
Two suits were wrinkled beyond recognition. My dyed
shoes had water streaks.

I had the suits cleaned and pressed for $7.56
(exhibit 1). The shoes were a different matter. The
shoe store said they couldn't be redyed. And since
I had just purchased those shoes, the shoe store
gave me a receipt for the original cost of the
shoes and the dying expense, $87.57 (exhibit 2).

Besides enclosing the two receipts, a copy of my
ticket to Houston (exhibit 3) is enclosed to verify
my flight into Houston on your airline.

Reasonable care suggests the luggage should have
been protected, too. The expenses I incurred would
not have happened except for lack of rain
protection by Andy Airlines. You should reimburse
me for the expenses.

This paragraph ends with why. We stated the solution in the first paragraph. Now the airline knows why our solution is the right one.

The closing paragraph—action
In the last paragraph restate the problem and then, as the last sentence, give the solution again. And, for added emphasis, underline the solution.

For instance, in the water damage example we just discussed, the final paragraph would read:

The lack of rain protection by Andy Airlines caused the damage
(problem). Reimburse me for the cleaning and shoe expenses.
They total $95.13 (solution).

That final paragraph asked for what we wanted in the rain damage situation. That request tells a story. In every complaint letter, be aggressive. Ask for what you want. It's the best way to get satisfaction.

Now let's recap the last paragraph. First, state the problem. Then put your solution last. You want the solution last because it's like the last impression—it's remembered.

The last paragraph is like a call to action in a sales letter. We're persuading another to meet our request. Now let's look at examples:

```
A computer foul-up must have caused this mistake (problem).
Crank up the computer and make the account right. Credit our
account for $310.00 (solution).
```

• • •

```
Our company ordered _____ with the understanding that we
could cancel after the first issue. Now you say we owe for the
entire subscription (problem). That's subscription by intimida-
tion. Expect no money and cancel the subscription (solution).
```

• • •

```
If we owed the higher premium, we'd pay it. But we don't
(problem). Acknowledge the policy change and reduce our
premium by $3,444.21 (solution).
```

To get those results you want, you must also be aware of other elements that can affect your request. Here are three:

1. *Time.* Either ask for a specific time limit or don't mention time at all.
   By including a time limit, you know whether the reader has taken action to correct the problem by a certain date. The time limit tells you if you need to follow-up.

   ```
   WRONG: Send the advertising agreements to me within a
          reasonable time.

   RIGHT: Send the advertising agreements to me by Friday,
          May 2.
   ```

   When you first complain, mentioning time is usually unnecessary. You generally omit any reference to it. Time becomes more important when a complaint drags on.

2. *Hope.* Never hope for agreement.
   Hope is a hedging word and shows weakness in language. Rather than a positive approach, you fudge and give the reader a chance to fudge back. If you want results, you must project strength with aggressive comments.

   ```
   WRONG: I hope you'll agree.

   RIGHT: Examine the information. Then credit the account
          for $235.50.
   ```

3. *Pleasantries.* Avoid pleasantries. Use action language.

   To me, *please* is like begging rather than insisting on action. And *thank you* is presumptuous and assumes the problem will be corrected. Neither pleasantry suggests strength, and strength is what your letter should communicate.

```
WRONG: Please give me your answer by next week. Thank you.

RIGHT: Give me your answer by telephone next week.
```

Complimentary close

Omit the complimentary close in all instances. The request for satisfaction should be the last item written.

Earlier we said we wanted our complaints to be impersonal. Omitting the complimentary close continues that thought.

Creative substitutions would be friendly. Being friendly might be presumptuous when we're complaining. We want solid negotiation, not buddy-buddy.

Postscript

The postscript is unnecessary. The solution in the last sentence of the letter should be the last thing written. Only after writing earlier letters and as a last resort should you even consider using the postscript. Then, as with a sales letter, you might use it for attention. Here's one you might use:

```
If I get a computer answer, you're compounding a felony. Who
wants to get an unsolicited bill and then be told by a com-
puter that you owe money?
```

Carbon copy

In a complaint, frustration often hits when no immediate results are gained. For instance, a computer mistake may make a solution seem impossible.

In these instances people involvement may give you your solution. On occasion a carbon copy to a division manager or a corporate president may give results. But use this approach as a last resort, not as an initial attack. As in a military battle, additional strength is held in reserve.

Hate letters

Sometimes a hate letter—or one that accuses—is used. Admittedly these letters occasionally get results. They get results, not because of the hate, but because the business wants to do the right thing.

I suggest that you avoid any type of hate letter. You want positive results that continue a good working relationship with your reader. (Besides, ruffling feathers only makes your job harder.)

SUMMARY

1. Always use the creative substitution for attention and omit any names on it.

2. In the first sentence of the first paragraph, create added attention by reinforcing the creative substitution.

3. Give a reasonable solution, not the problem, as the last sentence of the first paragraph.

4. Explain the problem history and include supporting data.

5. Justify the solution.

6. Ask for the solution again as the last sentence of the letter.

7. Omit the complimentary close.

8. Consider postscripts and carbon copies only as a last resort.

CHAPTER TEN

OPENINGS—USE A HAMMER

---

*Your first paragraph is the most important part of any letter.
Use it to get attention; make your reader want to continue.*

If you're hit over the head with a hammer, the impact gets your immediate attention (assuming you're still conscious!). Like that attention-getting hammer, your purpose in any opening is to get immediate attention. Consequently, you craft that first paragraph to grab readers so they want to continue.

Earlier we said that the attention created in the first five seconds of a letter often determines whether readers will continue. So it's imperative that we capture their interest immediately in the first paragraph.

Remember when you first got your driver's license. Any time your parents asked you to drive the car and run an errand, you probably eagerly leapt at the opportunity. Why? Because you were told something you wanted to hear.

Letter openings must act the same way. They must contain something readers want to hear. If not, letters become wasted effort that may be ignored or thrown away. But we don't want our letters thrown in the wastebasket. So we use techniques that capture immediate attention.

The most important technique I recommend is to couple the creative substitution with the first paragraph. That coupling increases substantially the effect of the first paragraph, because the creative substitution sets the stage for the entire letter. Its visual appeal, when coupled with the first paragraph, strengthens the letter's attention-getting power.

Here are examples that couple the creative substitution with an opening paragraph. Notice how they compliment each other:

1. Thanking for tickets.

WHAT A NICE TOUCH, ROGER:

```
Last week I received a courtesy invitation from you to SIX
FLAGS. What a delight. Both my wife and I needed an escape.
SIX FLAGS filled that beautifully.
```

2. A promotion for a magazine subscription.

YOU'RE A WINNER, MS. SCOTT:

```
Plain and simple. You were selected to receive a free gift
that could be worth as much as $21.95.
```

3. A promotion for a radial tire.

YOU'LL DISCOVER LUXURY MEETING PERFORMANCE:

```
The Road Runabout Radial now comes with a $38,000 stamp of ap-
proval. It's the tire of choice for ten imported and domestic
sports sedans and coupes — including the $38,000 1990 ORIK
sedan.
```

4. A reminder of value.

MILLIONS OF AMERICANS CAN'T READ THIS . . .

```
We're doing something about it. Our nationwide service
project, Ready to Read, is reaching out to people in our com-
munities who can't read or write.
```

5. A time-saving telephone.

BUY YOURSELF SOME TIME!!!

```
When there aren't enough hours in the day to cram in every-
thing you need to do, you need the _____ phone. This cel-
lular telephone goes wherever you go, freeing you from your
desk and ending games of phone tag.
```

6. A networking situation.

IT WAS NICE MEETING YOU, TOM . . .

```
. . . at the recent Chamber mixer. You sound like you have a
terrific job.
```

7. Answering an inquiry.

HERE IT IS, MS. BROWN:

```
You asked for information on the ZY-101. It's enclosed. You'll
find that the ZY-101 offers some unusual money-making oppor-
tunities.
```

TECHNIQUES THAT CAPTURE ATTENTION

Besides coupling the creative substitution with the first paragraph, we have a variety of techniques that make openings effective. Each has something in common. Each captures attention. And each tells readers what they want to hear.

Starting with an ah-ha statement

Ah-ha statements knock your socks off. Well, maybe not your socks, but they certainly jar your thinking. When you hear the sounds of an explosion or a car backfiring, the noise has your immediate attention. The noise awakens your emotions. *Ah-ha* statements also awaken your emotions. They create the unexpected or include startling facts and figures. Look at these examples:

- Imagine the postman arriving at your door with $1,000,000 for you. Imagine buying that dream home you always wanted. Or imagine having debt disappear and having money to make money.

- Take us to play. We're your perfect playmate. In fact, we fly you to playgrounds throughout the world.

- No down payment makes ORIK LeaseSmart very smart indeed for your next luxury automobile.

Beginning with a question

As we have seen, the question is a powerful attention-getting technique because it arouses curiosity. When you read a question, you want an answer. But the only way to obtain the answer is to read on. So what do you do? You read on.

When asking a question, you create a problem, and a problem needs an answer, a solution. So what do you do next? Immediately give an answer or a solution that suggests your product or idea is the right one. By supplying an answer, you've then started on a path to a meeting of the minds.

Now let's explore questions that create interest and the answers to those questions:

- What's ahead for 1992? The truth is, no one knows. Even the most skilled economists can't agree. That's where _____ Magazine comes in.

- Are you interested in public speaking? Have you achieved a successful track record in your industry over the last seven to ten years? Then you qualify to earn additional income through consulting. (The next paragraph promotes a consulting seminar.)

Answering a question or concern

When answering another's letter, common sense tells us that the reader wants to know about the question asked. So tell immediately about the information the reader is after. Come to the point.

Write answers, not runaround. These examples show what I mean:

WRONG: The repair to your building is a real concern. We've had our people preparing a bid for its repair. As you are aware, there are a lot of variables.
RIGHT: We bid $127,000 for the repair work to your building.

```
WRONG:  On September 2, you asked for information on whether
        we would be able to help. You gave us a good picture
        of what is needed.
RIGHT:  We can help.

WRONG:  With reference to your letter of November 3, you asked
        whether your order has been sent.
RIGHT:  Your sweatshirt order will be sent by air express on
        November 9.
```

Answering a request for information

When answering requests for information, let others know they are receiving information in the first sentence. Just as in answering questions, come to the point.

When others ask for information, they are creating their own problem—they want information. You have the solution they want. Tell them up front they will get the information. I underlined the answers below for emphasis so you can see that answers are always placed first.

```
WRONG:  This is in reference to your letter of May 1, when you
        asked us to send you information on our colored
        widgets. Enclosed is your requested information.
RIGHT:  Here it is. Enclosed is information you requested on
        our colored widgets.

WRONG:  Please be advised that our management committee has
        your recommendation under review. After consideration,
        a decision will be made. We will not, however, be able
        to get you the decision until Friday, May 1.
RIGHT:  You'll get management committee's decision about your
        recommendation on Friday, May 1.

WRONG:  It gives me great pleasure in being able to help you
        with your request for the membership directory. It's
        enclosed.
RIGHT:  Here's the membership directory you asked for. I'm glad
        I can help.
```

Incorporating a thank you

"Thank you" has a magic all its own, because it suggests nice things. Those words create a positive tone when you read them. So what do you do? You sit back and relax. You're comfortable, because the tone projects a warmth everyone likes. If you like "thank you," rest assured others do, too. When you can use a thank you, do.

```
• When you let us use your athletic facilities, you saved our
  lives. Thank you for your generous help.

• We couldn't have done it without you. The time you put in
  was Herculean. Thank you.
```

- What a wonderful gift. You should have seen how the office
  staff devoured your fruit basket. Thanks for thinking of us.

Complimenting the reader

Whenever anyone tells you that you did a fine job, that you were clever, or that your contribution was important, you react favorably. These compliments get your attention. When you compliment others in your letters, you can expect their favorable reaction and attention, too.

- Two plus two equals five (or even more) when you get involved. You make a significant contribution.
- Congratulations. Only you could have pulled that off so successfully.
- You did a superior job on that report. Keep up the good work.

Starting with a polite request or command

This no-frills approach comes to the point immediately. If readers know what is expected of them, they often do it. And if people are told at the start what they must do, then they continue to read to see if they have other things to do. Include "please" before your request.

- Please send us another $1.00 for your transcript. The fee
  is now $4.00. When we receive it, we'll rush Hard Knock
  University a copy.
- Please return the completed form in the courtesy envelope.
- Please complete the questions on pages 1 and 2. The sooner
  you complete and return the questionnaire, the sooner we can
  give you the answer.

Beginning with a name

Names arouse curiosity immediately, because people like to read about people. With a name others are hooked and want to keep on.

- Mr. Robert Perez of your office referred me to you. He told
  me you were looking for a program on time management.
- Your name was given to me by Phyllis Macy of Gold Unlimited.
- Send Sally Solution a copy of the report. She can help you
  get it approved.

Agreeing immediately

In customer service, agreeing immediately is always the way to go when you are correcting a complaint. Customers want to hear that they are right. Tell them. Don't waste their time recounting the facts. They already know them.

```
WRONG:  On January 3, you inquired whether your account had
        been overcharged. We made an investigation to deter-
        mine what should be done. It gives me great pleasure
        to tell you that your account has been credited for the
        $75.31 you asked for.
RIGHT:
```

**SKIPPING
APOLOGIES**

```
You're right. Your account has been credited
$75.31. The fact that you, Mr. G.W. Smith, were
charged for a bill of Mr. G. Wilson Smith's, tipped
us off to a billing conflict. You have helped us
ensure that this kind of billing error never occurs
again. Thanks.

To recognize your contribution, enclosed is a gift
certificate for $20.00. Part of your next purchase
is on us.
```

Any agreement is effective. When someone agrees with you in a letter, you continue reading. When there is good news, there must be more. Since you want others to continue, you use that approach, too. For instance, by agreeing with the reader, you make that person feel smart and important, on top of the world. With a feeling like that, you know the reader wants to continue reading.

```
What a smart decision, Dave. Becoming a consultant and your
own boss makes sense. With your experience and contacts,
you've already got a jump on cranking up a going concern.
```

Beginning with a resale

By letting others know that they've purchased a good product or service, you've flattered their smart decision. And since people like to hear they're smart, they continue.

```
● You have a reliable XYZ widget, and many neighbors think so,
  too.

● Your ORIK sports car has received many awards for quality.
  It has the quality you expect.

● You've got a winner. You have one of the best resale values
  in the industry.
```

Take advantage of these techniques. They give you effective openings. Remember though, only you can decide what is effective. For instance, in baseball when you're the hitter, you adjust to the pitch to get a hit. You must adjust with your letter openings, too. And by adjusting, expect a hit with your business letters.

CORRUPTING INFLUENCES IN THE OPENING

Look out! Poor writing habits can creep into the opening and undermine its strength. So keep your opening strong. To maintain this strength, avoid the corrupting influences of the empty opening, the buried conclusion, words that ruffle feathers, and the use of "I."

The empty opening

```
This letter refers to the correspondence that you wrote on
June 3.
```

When you see a letter start like this, you know you have a letter that starts with an empty opening, an opening that leaves out the attention step. By leaving out attention, the writer overlooks the reader, the person who should be put first.

Rather than including an interesting comment, the writer includes what he or she feels is important, not what the reader considers important. This omission could bring disaster to any letter and generate as much enjoyment as taking a cold shower.

When you receive a letter, you want to read what's important to you. That means you write that way and avoid the empty opening.

You identify the empty opening by its weak language. Generally, you find it with language that:

1. States the purpose.

2. Suggests interest.

3. Mentions the obvious.

4. Refers to prior correspondence.

First, by first telling the reader the purpose, you're only announcing an empty statement that fails to include attention and spice up the letter for the reader. Notice in this example how weak language can be transformed into powerful language:

```
EMPTY OPENING: The purpose of this letter is to tell you about
your advertising recommendation.

STRONG OPENING: Your advertising recommendation sold us.
```

Second, by suggesting interest, you are making a comment that may never come to pass in your letter. In fact, your message might bore the reader if you talk only about yourself or your product. You're leaving out what is important to the reader. Look at these contrasting openings:

```
EMPTY OPENING: This letter will be interesting to you.

STRONG OPENING: Picture this vacation escape.
```

The obvious never persuades, because it doesn't create attention. Rather, tell readers what they want to hear:

```
EMPTY OPENING: This is in answer to your letter of May 2,
where you requested additional information.

STRONG OPENING: Here's the information you wanted.
```

Finally, by referring to prior correspondence, a letter creates a void, because it omits the attention step. Yes, it provides a reference that may be important for legal identification. In fact, legal requirements may dictate a reference. But no rule of law says you have to confuse the reader with legal jargon or write like a lawyer.

When you need a reference, either put it in a subject line or in the first sentence without an empty opening. These examples show how to make the empty opening disappear when a references is needed:

```
EMPTY OPENING: This letter acknowledges receipt of the 1992 TV
contract you sent us on October 5.

STRONG OPENING: The 1992 TV contracts arrived in ample time.

SUBJECT LINE: SUBJECT: 1992 TV contracts.
```

There is no trick to eliminating empty openings. You eliminate them by using the attention-getting techniques discussed earlier. Notice how the empty openings vanish in these next examples when attention-getting techniques are used:

```
WRONG: This letter has reference to our conversation of
       yesterday. You mentioned the possibility of lunch on
       Tuesday (reference).
RIGHT: Can you make lunch on Tuesday (a question)?

WRONG: The purpose of this letter is to tell you of the fine
       job you did (purpose).
RIGHT: Your efforts were tremendous (complimenting the
       reader).

WRONG: Reference is made to your letter of May 1, when you
       asked about our travel plans (reference).
WRONG: I was glad to receive your letter of May 1, when you
       asked about our travel plans (reference).
RIGHT: Yes, we plan to travel by air (answering a previous
       question).
```

The buried conclusion

To start a car, you turn the ignition. To start a fire, you light it. In both examples you do first things first. Likewise, to start a letter, you do first things first; you come to the point.

When you receive a letter, you want to know what it's about. When a letter comes to the point, you do find out immediately. If, however, you have a buried conclusion, you have to search for the letter's purpose and may lose interest.

Look at some of the letters you receive. When they have a buried conclusion, they may seem like a maze, and you might wonder if you will ever finish them. And while struggling through those letters, you could ask yourself, "What's wanted?" or "Who should do it?" Somehow the conclusion never seems to come.

Oh, a letter might come from a vice president, and you know you must read it. If you had a choice, though, you'd rather not. Why? Because the letter wastes your time. Rather than coming to the point, you waste effort trying to understand the message.

While the buried conclusion can hit anyone, the inexperienced writer makes this mistake most often. Suppose the inexperienced writer makes a proposal to increase the cars the company owns by twelve to give added flexibility.

What do you find? You find an opening that says something about the time delays because of lack of cars and the burdens they cause. Buried down in the recommendation is the proposal for twelve new cars. This approach forces you to plow through the letter and dig for the conclusion. You shouldn't have to.

Since you want to save time when you read, you look for the meat of the recommendation at the start. You hope to see a firm proposal (like "twelve new cars") at the beginning. Even better, you prefer the recommendation be underlined. Coming to the point couldn't be clearer. You would then see something like this:

```
For increased flexibility for our employees who use cars, we
should add twelve new cars to our fleet of cars.
```

As the boss you want solutions, answers, results, and conclusions. You want the information up front so you don't waste time trying to find what's needed. You want the first paragraph to tell you what you want to know.

Then if you're interested in the first paragraph, you can read on. The supporting facts become important. And more important, the recommendation is focused with the conclusion first.

When you're not interested, then the focused first paragraph makes it easy for you not to read the rest of the letter. You don't have to become mired in the details. And by reading only the first paragraph, you save valuable time for other projects.

As a professional or a business executive, you can't afford either receiving or writing letters that have buried conclusions. Those letters waste both time and money.

So avoid the buried conclusion. Give your writing the clear thinking it deserves. Come to the point whenever you make a recommendation.

Words that ruffle feathers
Another problem arises whenever you use words that irritate or insult readers. Those nasty words either turn them off so they fail to read your material or turn them against you or your company. In effect, these words misfire and project an irritating arrogance or insincerity. Examples tell the story:

1. Accusing the reader.

> WRONG: "You claim," "you state," or "you promised."

This language immediately accuses readers and puts them on the defensive. They are biting, because they imply incorrect information from the customer or reader. They're red flag words; they turn readers into raging bulls.

```
RIGHT: If the repair could be done, action would be
       taken.
```

2. Stating the obvious.

```
WRONG: "As you know."
```

Why state the obvious? Readers rarely want to be told something they already know.

```
RIGHT: With these facts and figures, help is possible.
```

3. Sounding argumentative.

```
WRONG: You "seem to think," "contend," or "allege."
```

These words suggest an argument. We don't want an argument or a quarrel. We want a settlement.

```
RIGHT: The solution is difficult.
```

4. Asking foolish questions.

```
WRONG: Do you want to double your money in a year?
```

This foolish question implying something no one can guarantee.

```
RIGHT: Increase your odds.
```

5. Insulting the customer.

```
WRONG: Reliable people pay promptly.
```

This implied insult suggests that your customers are unreliable. Instead, encourage them to live up to your expectations. Unpleasant language provides little cooperation. Warnings of fact are more likely to bring results. In a collection letter people expect consequences, not insults.

```
RIGHT: We expect prompt payment.
```

6. Implying doubt as to the reader's intelligence.

```
WRONG: Surely you must understand the need to pay your
       bill.
```

```
WRONG: We can't understand why your check hasn't ar-
       rived.
```

It you want to irritate readers, just tell them they "must understand" or that you "can't understand." This language is like telling others that they are foolish.

> RIGHT: Clear your bill.

7. Blaming the reader for a mistake.

> WRONG: "It is impossible to tell," "you failed to men-
> tion," "you neglected to say."

This language tells readers they are stupid. If you want to lose customers, these comments succeed.

> RIGHT: So we can complete your order, please tell us
> what color you want.

The use of "I"

Avoid using "I" to start a letter. Use the "you approach" and put the other person first. "I" suggests ego. When you start using "I" in your letters, you put yourself first at the expense of the reader. And that approach weakens the effectiveness of your letters. Why make them less effective with "I"?

Good listeners put themselves in the background and make others feel important. Just as a good listener puts the speaker first, so too your letters should put the reader first. You should be in the background. These examples show what I mean:

> WRONG: I'm enclosing the production schedule to guide you.
> RIGHT: Here is the production schedule you wanted to help you.
>
> WRONG: I think you'll like my recommendation on productivity.
> RIGHT: The recommendation covers productivity.
>
> WRONG: I'd like to acknowledge your nice comments.
> RIGHT: You comments were great. Thank you.

"I" creates another problem; it often injects unnecessary opinion. And if you inject an opinion, you miss an opportunity to make a statement positive. The battleship becomes a toy boat. These next examples start with an opinion and then eliminate the opinion words "I think that":

> WRONG: I think that we need to cover travel expenses.
> RIGHT: We need to cover travel expenses.
>
> WRONG: I think that we should apply the money to the loan.
> RIGHT: We should apply the money to the loan.
>
> WRONG: I think that you made a fine recommendation.
> RIGHT: You made a fine recommendation.

But don't think you should always drop "I." It's often very useful. When an opinion is necessary, only "I" gives it. For example, when asking for help, you might say, "I need your help." Or if relating a story, you would inject "I" and say, "I remember what it was like as a college student. I found . . ."

When you write friends and acquaintances, they want to hear about you and expect the friendliness of "I." In these instances, only "I" gives the flavor of from-me-to-you. For instance, "I" gives a necessary opinion in this example: "I liked the way you handled the management presentation."

Important people also use "I" to express an opinion. If a president of a corporation expresses an opinion, you take notice. If politicians think they can help, "I" lets them give their opinion. Here the opinion serves them.

Another use of "I" helps eliminate a stuffy style. For example, words like "the author" or "the writer" serve no one, because they project a stuffy style. In these instances, "I" becomes important. Here you substitute the stuffy words with "I" to project a friendly tone.

If "I" fits, use it, but use it sparingly.

SUMMARY

Use the tools or writing techniques of the effective opening to get that attention.

1. The most important paragraph is the first. Use it for attention so the reader will continue.

2. Techniques for openings.

   a. Couple the creative substitution with the first paragraph.

   b. Start with an *ah-ha* statement.

   c. Begin with a question.

   d. Answer a question or concern.

   e. Answer a request for information.

   f. Incorporate a thank you.

   g. Compliment the reader.

   h. Start with a polite request or command.

   i. Begin with a name.

   j. Agree immediately.

   k. Begin with a resale.

3. Avoid corrupting influences in the opening.

   a. The empty opening.

   b. The buried conclusion.

   c. Words that ruffle feathers.

d. The use of "I."

    1) Improper use.

        a) Suggesting ego.

        b) Giving unnecessary opinion.

        c) Weakening recommendations.

    2) Exceptions.

        a) Giving necessary opinions.

        b) Writing friends and acquaintances.

        c) Comments by important people.

        d) Substituting for stuffy words.

CHAPTER ELEVEN

CLOSINGS—USE THE HAMMER AGAIN

Your last paragraph lets your reader remember your message.
Use closing techniques to make your last thought potent.

GENERAL

From your closing paragraph, readers receive a final impression of you or your company. And since you want a favorable impression, what do you include in your closing to help your letters? Do you close with the same language in a denial as you do in a request for help? What do you say if you compliment someone? How do you create goodwill? What's required to sell a product?

We'll explore these questions. But first, let's look at empty closings you should always avoid. They undermine the previous work you've developed in your letter.

THE EMPTY CLOSING

Many letters have empty closings that add needless language that bores both readers and writers.

That last paragraph you just read sounds fine, but what does it mean? How do you identify the empty closing? You identify it with a simple test: "Does the language add anything to the letter?"

When empty language adds nothing to your letters, you are weakening them. To strengthen your letters, you must know how to identify that kind of language so you avoid it. The discussions that follow show the characteristics of three empty closing approaches. All weaken your message.

1. Using hedging words.

2. Stating the obvious.

3. Asking questions.

Using hedging words

Hedging words let readers avoid commitment to your idea. This "weasle language" suggests either an option to get out or indifference on your part. We certainly don't want that.

Let me explain hedging language with a letter's closing paragraph from someone who wanted me to work with him on a writing book. His letter helped me decide I didn't want to work with him.

Here's what his closing comments were. I consider them the finest examples I have ever seen on how not to write a call to action:

> <u>Please</u> send your proposal for writing the book <u>at your ear-</u>
> <u>liest convenience.</u> <u>If</u> you have any <u>questions</u> or comments about
> our products or about this opportunity, please give me a call.
> <u>Thank you</u> very much for your <u>consideration</u>.

Let me address the words that trouble me.

PLEASE

In a call to action paragraph, avoid pleasantries like "please." In my opinion, that word is like begging. Oh, I agree that the word is one of the magic words, but scrap it in a selling letter.

Rather, use imperative sentences that suggest action. In his letter all he needed was "send."

AT YOUR CONVENIENCE

If you were a banker and I had a loan at your bank, what would paying "at your convenience" mean? To you it would probably mean this month. But not to me. I might think of it as a year, five years, never.

Rather than use "at your convenience," use a specific time like "at the end of the month," "September 2," or "by next month." That time limit creates a deadline and puts a sense of urgency in your request.

IF

What's wrong with that word? Nothing, if it is used in a first paragraph. But never use it in a call to action. It gives the reader an option to get out.

For instance, when I write, "If you're ready to do business," the other person has an option to deny being ready. Instead, use "When you're ready." Assume that person will do business with you.

QUESTIONS

I don't know about you, but questions remind me of problems, and I have enough of those. So rather than the phrase, "If you have any questions," substitute language like "For added information," or "For more information."

THANK YOU

Suppose I asked you if you had $5.00 in your purse or billfold. Suppose further that you said yes. Then suppose I said, "Thank you for giving it to me." You'd think I was crazy. Of course, you wouldn't give me the $5.00. I was presumptuous for thanking you for something you didn't do and didn't plan to do.

Likewise, don't thank others in a call-to-action paragraph. It doesn't persuade. Rather, reserve "thank you" for praising others for something they did, not for what they didn't do.

Instead of the weak "thank you," use imperative sentences to persuade. Notice the contrast in the examples that follow.

```
WRONG: Thank you for your contribution.
RIGHT: Help support the United Way.

WRONG: Thank you in advance for giving your time.
RIGHT: Experience the satisfaction.

WRONG: Thank you for the help you'll give.
RIGHT: Join the effort.
```

FOR YOUR CONSIDERATION

Did he want me to consider getting the proposal to him or did he want me to send it to him? I think he wanted me to send him the proposal. Moral: drop "consideration" from your vocabulary in a call-to-action paragraph.

Here are other examples of hedging and suggested corrections:

```
WRONG: Trusting that you are in agreement with this de-
       cision, I hope you will sign the contract.
```

We have a double whammy of hedging, "trusting" and "I hope."

```
RIGHT: Let me know you agree. Sign the contract.
```

No hedging here.

```
WRONG: I want to thank you in advance for support.
```

Use "thank you" for something that has happened, not for something that may never happen. Thanking in advance presumes a favorable response that may never come.

```
RIGHT: Support the effort.
```

When you want something, ask for it.

```
WRONG: I hope you will look at the _____.
```

"I hope" never persuades. Replace that language with an imperative sentence or sentences.

```
RIGHT: Examine the _____ and discover.

WRONG: Your possible interest is appreciated.
```

This language asks the customer to do nothing. If you expect nothing, learn to have your expectations filled.

```
RIGHT: Take advantage of it.
```

Stating the obvious

Another form of an empty closing states the obvious. When your reader or customer already knows what you are talking about, why mention the obvious? Here are examples:

```
WRONG: In conclusion, I want to remind you of the impor-
       tance of the next meeting (the obvious).
```

Whenever you see language like "in conclusion" or "in summary," you often see the obvious. The writer is announcing the message rather than telling it.

```
RIGHT: Attend the meeting.
```

Importance should have already been discussed. Use the closing to request action.

```
WRONG: As you know, the report must be completed by
       March 1.
```

If the reader already knows, why mention those words? Besides that language puts others on the defensive if there is a question of meeting the deadline.

```
RIGHT: Complete the report by March 1.
```

This sentence suggests action.

Asking questions

Questions are effective for openings because we immediately supply an answer for readers. With our answers we then say that our product or service is the way to go.

In a closing, however, we don't have time to provide an answer. A question gives the reader an escape from our appeal. And an escape only means that we reduce our chances of success with a letter.

In a call to action, we want the reader to act on our message. We don't want to give the reader an option to get out. Why spend effort developing a persuasive letter and then close with a question that lets readers or customers off the hook? It doesn't make sense. If we want results, let's ask for them.

Look at the examples that follow. The first part of the example asks a question. Notice the possible answers that follow those questions. Also notice the difference between questions and the suggested replacements that use imperative sentences.

```
WRONG: Don't you agree that it's time to take this im-
       portant step?
```

"No. They've got nerve telling me when to act."

```
RIGHT: Try it. All you need to do is return the reply
       card. You'll be delighted with the results you
       get.
```

```
WRONG: Won't you call today?
```

"No. Why should I? You'll just give me a hard sell."

```
RIGHT: Find out how easy it is to get your office
       cleaned quickly and professionally. Call CLEANER
       INC. today at 111-1111. Then ask about our FREE
       first visit.
```

```
WRONG: May we hear from you soon?
```

"No. Are you crazy? All you want me to do is spend money."

```
RIGHT: Start your journey today with THE WONDERS OF THE
       SAHARA. Spark your imagination with a 10-day FREE
       trial of our introductory volume. Just return the
       enclosed certificate. Your trial volume will be
       on its way.
```

DIFFERENT LETTER TYPES REQUIRE DIFFERENT CLOSINGS

We've just talked about what we shouldn't do when we end a letter. Now let's look at what we should do.

In previous chapters we addressed three kinds of letters, the "no," "yes," and "persuasive" letters. Each requires a different closing.

- "No" letter (a friendly close and hope).
- "Yes" letter (recalls the good comments and looks to the future).
- "Persuading" letter (a call to action).

Let's examine examples of these types of letters to show the difference between them.

The first closing paragraph we'll look at is for a "no" letter. It's a denial of credit. Because of the denial, we anticipate a negative response and want to neutralize it. To do that, our last paragraph leaves the reader with a friendly thought and a feeling of hope.

For instance, after denying credit because the applicant has no job, be encouraging and make the reader feel better. Then offer an element of hope:

```
In the meantime, we welcome you as a cash customer. When your
credit situation changes, let us know. We'll send you a credit
application.
```

This closing paragraph gives an alternative to credit. Then it suggests a future change of circumstances. Because this letter ends on a friendly note and offers hope, we should help ourselves. A curt rejection would not.

In a "yes" letter closing paragraph, our job is to make the good feeling even stronger. So we reinforce what we've already said and then look to the future. Here's a closing congratulations paragraph to a person recently selected as president of a Chamber of Commerce:

```
Your managerial expertise will strengthen the Chamber. Con-
gratulations again. I know we can look forward to positive
results with you at the helm.
```

If you received a letter with this closing paragraph, you'd feel great. That last paragraph not only strengthens what's already been said, it looks to the future in a most favorable light.

In a persuading letter the closing paragraph is different. We want results, so it contains a call to action. For instance, this next closing paragraph is from a contribution request. It is persuading someone to give.

```
The Multiple Sclerosis Society helps others help themselves.
Join me in giving. Support this effort with a check.
```

This persuading example uses imperative sentences that start with "join" and "support." In addition, it uses a call to action and asks the reader to do something, to write a check. Whenever we persuade, always use imperative sentences in the closing paragraph to get the reader to act.

These denial, congratulations, and contribution closings required different approaches for the closing paragraph. When you expect a negative response ("no"), end on a friendly note and include an element of hope. When you expect a positive response ("yes"), close by recalling earlier comments and looking favorably to the future. When you expect action from your reader, ask for it.

Now let's discuss in more detail the closing paragraphs for specific "no," "yes," and "persuading" letters.

CLOSINGS FOR THE "NO" LETTER

When you write a "no" letter, you're writing others about news they'd rather not hear. You anticipate a negative response and want to shift that reaction to at least a neutral reaction.

A back pain could remind you of an injury. A dented fender could remind you of an accident. But the closing of a "no" letter should never remind the reader of bad news. Rather, you must be pleasant.

Whatever you do, never talk about the unpleasant idea in the last paragraph. Reserve this paragraph for something positive. Help readers have a favorable image of you and your company when they finish your letter. By dwelling on the positive, you leave the reader with the impression you want, a positive one.

For instance, when your firm denies a charitable organization's request for money, you want to end your letter on a favorable or encouraging note. Do that in your closing paragraph. Then you might say:

- Your medical reserch helps everyone. Keep up the fine work.

- The unselfish magic of the United Way makes it happen. Continue that wonderful people help.

- Your hospital care works wonders in our community. Keep it up.

Remember, people respond in kind. If you're cheerful, you give your reader a reason to be cheerful. So be friendly in the "no" closing. Project a favorable image.

You often project that image by saying good luck in your closing. Since people like to be told good luck or to be wished success, tell them. Even though you say no, counter the negative comment with a positive statement. The old saying, "A half a loaf of bread is better than none," definitely applies here.

- You've got good credentials. Good luck with your job search.

- I wish we could use you now. Meanwhile, good luck with your effort.

- Good luck with your program. Maybe in a few months circumstances will change. Give me a call in July and we'll talk.

Many times others ask for information or help you don't have. Rather than end with a cold "no," suggest other sources that do have the information or that can help. When you do, you leave an impression that you're a good person.

- The American Medical Association should have the information you need. Contact them at . . .

- Your U.S. Representative, Joe Johnson, should be able to help you with that request. Write him at . . .

When you receive an order for a product you no longer carry, you have to say no to that order. But don't stop with no. Turn this no into an opportunity. Suggest something else; suggest a different product. With this approach, you're turning a problem into an opportunity. Just because you say no, that doesn't suggest you are unable to sell. It just means that you sell harder . . . and smarter.

- Our new product should fill your needs. I'll see you at lunch a week from Friday. We'll talk about it then.

- This is one of our biggest sellers. Examine it. I'll call you on <u>Friday, June 14</u> and explore how it might fill your needs.

When saying no, you often offer a counterproposal. By taking this approach, you can say what you can do, not what you can't do. And by giving an alternative, you capture a positive feeling.

- I'd like to talk to your club next month, but I have another engagement. My assistant can, however. If you'd like him to speak, call me.

- The enclosure tells what we can do and what we offer. Review it and discover some of the latest technology being offered today. I'll call you Thursday, May 1, to see how we might work together.

In a no response, leave out the creative substitution. Just go from the body of the letter to the signature.

Complimentary closes like "Sincerely" and "Yours truly" add nothing to the letter. In addition, a friendly creative substitution may leave a sense of false expectations and being too chummy.

When saying no, we should try to be impersonal. We've already excluded the salutation to be impersonal. Let's use that same approach for the complimentary close.

CLOSINGS FOR THE "YES" LETTER

The "yes" letter always generates favorable goodwill. With it, you expect a positive reaction. Your job, then, is to strengthen that positive reaction, so your closing leaves the reader with a warm fuzzy feeling.

Your first step in a "yes" closing is to start the last paragraph with a first sentence or two that recalls the good news stated earlier. People like reminders of nice results. Say the nice reminders and leave the reader pleased.

- Your positive attitude and help gave us all necessary strength.

- The information in your speech was great. You covered many original thoughts.

- When your ideas arrive next week, you'll help our position.

After recalling the good news, continue with a final thought that looks to the future. For instance, whenever you compliment someone, be sure the last sentence uses language like these examples:

- Your positive attitude and help gave us all necessary strength. <u>I look forwrd to working with you again.</u>

- The information in your speech was great. You offered many original thoughts. <u>Keep up the good work.</u>

- When you ideas arrive next week, you'll help our position. <u>Keep those valuable comments coming.</u>

A thank-you letter is a "yes" letter that requires special comment. If you've said thank you in the first paragraph, you don't have to include the thank you in the last paragraph. I repeat, *you don't have to include thank you in the last paragraph.*

How come? Thank you recalls good news, and we want good news remembered. Yes, but rather than include thank you in the last paragraph, include it as a creative substitution, as the complimentary close. Then the last paragraph makes a positive statement about the deed, looks to the future, and still lets you use the creative substitution. These examples show what I mean:

```
Your art gift to the museum was superb. I look forward to your
continuing as an art patron.
```

THANKS AGAIN FOR YOUR SUPPORT

• • •

```
Your suggestions really helped. Keep them coming.
```

THANKS AGAIN,

• • •

```
No one does it like you do. Keep up the good work.
```

THANKS FOR THE HELP!!!

While I recommend omitting thank you in the last paragraph, that approach is not an absolute. In some instances you may want to include thank you in the last paragraph. Then your last paragraph and creative substitution look like this:

```
Your efforts created excitement. Thanks, Joe. I look forward
to doing more business with you.
```

HAVE A GREAT 1992

• • •

```
The report generated attention. Thanks. Keep those fine re-
ports coming.
```

SEE YOU TUESDAY,

• • •

```
Other customers must be as pleased as I am. Your service was
spectacular. Thanks for your understanding repair work. You
can feel certain that I will not only return to your firm,
I'll recommend you to others.
```

KEEP UP YOUR WONDERFUL WORK!!!

CLOSINGS FOR THE PERSUADING LETTER

The letter closing for the persuasive letter has one purpose—to get your reader to take action. Without getting the reader to act, why write the letter?

You've captured attention, told why the product or service is needed, used data to support the need, and then convinced the reader of the need. Each of these elements is needed in a persuasive letter. Without a closing appeal for action, however, the greatest persuasive approach fails.

Since what you read last is generally remembered best, logic dictates that persuading closings include the request for action. For example, if you want to sell the government your office supplies, you don't let them off the hook and "hope" or "wish" for an order. You don't end with pleasantries. Instead, you tell them what they need to do to place the order:

```
Examine the catalogue. Then determine which products you need,
complete the order form, and return it in the return envelope.
When we receive it, expect delivery within seven days.
```

If you're a wholesaler and sell cameras, you probably tell about quality, warranties, why it's important to have product, how buyers can make more money, or tips on how the customer would react to some selling ideas. But the total selling package is only complete if you get the other person to act. So you say something at the end like:

```
Let us know how many cameras you want. Complete the order form
and return it in the return envelope. We'll rush your order
right to you.
```

The call to action is the climax, the peak of your sales effort. When you climb a mountain, you want to reach the top. When you sell, reaching the top is getting the order. You can only get that order with a specific request, a call to action.

```
● To get this sample, return the enclosed order card.

● You'll receive further benefits if you send your check to
  us by the end of the month.

● The sale includes everything in the store. Come in tomorrow
  and take advantage of the reduced prices.
```

The call to action requires more than a request for action. You must make response easy. For instance, you make response easy with an enclosed order form, when others can pay by credit card, or with a toll-free telephone number. In effect, you are providing tools to make response easy and are making the act effortless.

Another form of ease of action is the self-addressed, stamped envelope. There the sellers are saying, "It's free to answer. Do." They want you to answer; they know the importance of ease of action. When you want information or an order, you should follow this approach, too.

Many times the call to action includes a time element. If appropriate, be specific and include a definite time for action. Whenever time is important, say so. Don't fudge and hope you'll get an answer. And to get added emphasis, underline the date. In some instances, you may even want to highlight the date with a marker.

These next examples show the difference between being general and specific:

```
GENERAL: Get your order to us within a reasonable time.

SPECIFIC: Get your order to us by Monday, April 20.

GENERAL: "At your convenience..." or "As soon as convenient..."

SPECIFIC: Put the information in the mail by Friday, October 1.
```

That specific time should also be used when you tell someone you will call them. In those instances, howeve, I recommend more than just including a specific date. Besides underlining it to get attention, type the date on your business card ("Will call Monday, April 2.") Then attach your business card to the letter before you mail it.

Here's what you've done. You've organized your schedule. The recipient of your letter will assume immediately that you are organized. And many times when you call, you'll hear comments like, "Oh, you said you would call," "You're in my tickler file," or "Your name is on my calendar."

We look for an edge when we call. Use the specific date in your letters and on your business card as an edge to help you get your calls completed.

SUMMARY
To keep the attention you've generated, use the attention hammer again in the closing. Help others remember what you write.

1. Avoid the empty closing.

    a. Avoid hedging language.

    b. Avoid stating the obvious.

    c. Avoid asking questions.

2. Different letter types require different closings.

3. Closings for the "no" letter.

    a. Be cheerful and project a favorable image. Talk about something other than the unpleasant idea.

    b. Suggestions.

        1) Express good wishes for the program or project.

        2) End with a suggestion of other sources.

        3) Sell a different product.

        4) Use a counterproposal saying what you can do.

4. Closings for the "yes" letter.

    a. Recall the good news stated earlier in the letter.

    b. After recalling the good news, look to the future.

5. Closings for the "persuading" letter.

    a. Make a request for action.

    b. Make response easy.

    c. Consider time limits.

SAMPLE BUSINESS LETTERS

INSURANCE SETTLEMENT

SITUATION: Jerry Adams was recently killed in an automobile accident. His insurance agent must write a letter of sympathy and let the surviving wife know she'll receive $100,000.

This example makes it a point not to apologize for the death.

Mary,

Jerry was a special person. Ever time I came in contact with him, he had that knack to make me feel good. I miss him. I know you do too.

He loved you very much and anticipated your need in case anything happened to him. You're the beneficiary of a $100,000.00 insurance policy.

But we need your help to get those funds to you. Please send us a copy of the death certificate. Use the enclosed envelope. The sooner you send that to us the sooner we can send you the policy proceeds.

I'm glad we can help.

ACCEPTING A SPEAKING ENGAGEMENT

SITUATION: Fred Johnson, the president of the local United Way, has been asked to speak for the anniversary dinner for a local Kiwanis club. He told the club's president, a personal friend, he'd be glad to.

This letter confirms the details of the acceptance and uses the "Yes Plan" to create a good feeling.

YOU CAN COUNT ON ME, BILL:

I'd be glad to talk for your anniversary dinner next month on Thursday, April 13. The dinner starts at 7:00pm. I'll be there.

My talk will be entitled, THE MAGIC OF COMMUNITY SERVICE. That talk will be like talking to the choir. Kiwanis members do so much for the community. You can be especially proud of what you do with supporting the homeless.

Your reputation for community service is outstanding. Keep up your fine work.

SEE YOU APRIL 13 . . .

ACKNOWLEDGING A FIRST ORDER

SITUATION: The XYZ Corporation provides top of the line visual presentation needs. Whether printing, slides, or overheads, XYZ feels they can give the best.

After the work for a first order has been completed, XYZ sends a letter that acknowledges the first order and reaffirms that the customer can expect the best.

IT'S A WIN-WIN SITUATION, WAYNE:

You receive winning graphic support. We win a valuable customer. Thanks for your first order and for letting us do business with you.

As a new client, I wish to personally extend to you our commitment to the quality look you want for your corporate presentations. Appearances count, and we intend to consistently help you create that positive appearance you expect.

Equipped with the most advanced graphics technology available, you'll find that professional image you're looking for. We feel we can give you the best. As your account representative, I'm confident we'll make a difference for _____.

Wayne, I'm excited to be working with you. When you need visual presentation help again, let me know. I'm only a phone call away.

EXPECT A VISUAL EDGE WITH XYZ . . .

CONGRATULATIONS TO A COLLEAGUE

SITUATION: A close friend and colleague has been selected as the "Woman of the Year" by the Chamber of Commerce. As a friend you want to write a letter that cements an already good business relationship.

This is the kind of letter that never has to be written. After all, its message could be handled by telephone. The impact of the letter, however, is permanent. The impact of a phone call is fleeting.

WAY TO GO, ANNE:

You're living proof that cream rises to the top. You've always had a reputation as a top performer. The "Woman of the Year" award you received at last night's banquet just adds to that reputation. Congratulations.

Having you as a colleague and friend has been a joy. Whenever there was a rough spot, you somehow seemed to smooth it out. You have always been terrific.

If anyone in our city deserved that award, it was you. You're special. I'm glad to count you as a friend. Keep up your good work for both your company and the community.

CALL ME . . . .

ANSWERING A REQUEST FOR MEMBERSHIP INFORMATION

SITUATION: Mr. Tony Williams has asked for membership information about the American Society for Training and Development and about the local chapter.

Since a positive response is expected, this informational letter follows the "Yes Plan."

HERE'S THE INFORMATION, TONY . . .

. . . that you requested about the American Society for Training and Development. It includes these items:

— our recent newsletter, BULLETIN,

— membership application, chapter

— membership application, National

— information about both the local chapter and National.

We're excited that you are considering joining us. We meet the first Wednesday of every month at the Plaza Hotel (Beach & I-20) at 11:30am to 1:00pm and have a short program by a training professional about the latest in training.

The BULLETIN you have shows our next luncheon meeting will be Wednesday, December 2. The program will be THE GAMES PEOPLE PLAY. Join us. You'll like what you see.

SEE YOU THERE . . .

P.S. You'll need a reservation for lunch. Call Juanita Jones at 111-1111 for that.

WELCOMING NEW CHAMBER MEMBERS

SITUATION: After joining the Chamber, the president of the Chamber writes and welcomes the new members

YOU'LL LIKE YOUR DECISION, MR. _____ . . .

. . . about joining the _____ CHAMBER OF COMMERCE. You'll find a valuable organization to help your business grow.

And the sooner you get involved in CHAMBER activities, the sooner you'll discover the benefits of _____ CHAMBER membership. To help your involvement get started, you're invited to attend the following CHAMBER events:

* <u>New Member Orientation (VIP Coffee)</u> — at which you can learn what we do and the many ways you can become involved. The next VIP Coffee will be Thursday, June 14, at the Chamber office.

* <u>Membership Luncheon</u> — Tuesday, June 19, 1999, 12 noon at the _____ Hotel, 111 Main Street. Our Chairman of the Board will be the featured speaker.

* <u>After Hours Business Card Exchange</u> — Tuesday, June 12, at 5:30-7:30pm at the _____ Hotel, 1234 West Avenue. Tickets are $5 for members and their guests, $10 for non-members.

Take advantage of CHAMBER activities. You'll be glad you did.

WELCOME TO THE CHAMBER . . .

P.S. Be sure to attend the "After Hours Business Card Exchange" on _____ at the _____ Hotel. It's a great way to make valuable contacts.

COLLECTION—FIRST REMINDER
Giving customer benefit of the doubt

SITUATION: A customer with a good credit rating has failed to pay a current bill.

February 20, 1999

THE XYZ COMPANY
Box 111
Commerce, GA 30599

SUBJECT: Order AMO-54168

The charge of $532.18 for <u>name of product</u> is now due. A copy
of the invoice is enclosed.

Because of your past record of prompt payment, you probably
overlooked the charge. To bring your account up to date,
please mail us your check for those _____ today.

Use the courtesy envelope for your payment.

                    U-235 Unlimited, Inc.

PAST DUE: $532.18

COLLECTION—SECOND REMINDER
Asking for payment or reason for delay

SITUATION: A customer with a good credit rating has failed to pay a current bill. A collection note was sent after 40 days. The charge remains unpaid ten days later. Now we again ask for payment or an explanation of why the account hasn't been paid.

```
THE XYZ COMPANY
Box 111
Commerce, GA 30599

SUBJECT: Order AMO-54168

On February 20, a past due notice was sent to you asking for
payment of $532.18 for _____. The bill remains
outstanding. Let us know why. Perhaps it was merely an
oversight. We do want you to clear your account. Take a moment
now to write us a check for $532.18 and send it in the
courtesy envelope.

If, however, there are other reasons we should know about,
please tell us. If you are in temporary financial
difficulties, we'll try and work something out.

But whatever you do, let us know. Let's get the account
settled. Our toll-free number: 1-800-222-2222.


                                        F.B. Smith


PAST DUE: $532.18
```

COLLECTION—THIRD REMINDER
Protecting credit record

SITUATION: A customer with a good credit rating has failed to pay a current bill. Two collection notices have been ignored. Now we again ask for payment and aim our appeal at credit reputation and the importance of maintaining the firm's credit line.

March 13, 1999

THE XYZ COMPANY
Box 111
Commerce, GA 30599

SUBJECT: Order AMO-54168

It's one of our most important assets. With it we can order supplies, take trips, and purchase equipment. It is credit. It's something we all value.

Your credit record is as much a part of your business as making a sale. Can you afford to let it slip? I don't think so. Yet you are now risking your credit record by not paying your overdue bill.

On two previous occasions we have written and asked for payment of $532.18, the amount owed to us. No reply has been made. This continued silence on your part undermines your credit standing. Failure to pay forces us to report this to our credit bureau.

Keep your credit record intact. Only you can ensure a favorable credit reputation that gives you the continued confidence of buying on credit. Send us your check today. You'll be glad you did. Then, we, along with your other suppliers, will be able to continue serving you.

Send us a check for $532.18 and reestablish your favorable credit rating. Get the check to us by Monday, March 28. We can then clear your credit history of any reference of slow pay.

Our toll-free number: 1-800-222-2222.

F.B. Smith

PAST DUE: $532.18

COLLECTION—FINAL REMINDER

SITUATION: A customer with a good credit rating has failed to pay a current bill. Three collection notices have been ignored. Now we again ask for payment within a week or the account will be placed in the hands of an attorney.

```
March 29, 1999

THE XYZ COMPANY
Box 111
Commerce, GA 30599

SUBJECT: Order AMO-54168

On three separate occasions you were reminded to pay your past
due account. Payment has still not been received.

Unless we receive your payment of $532.18 by Monday, April 8,
your account will be placed in the hands of our attorney for
collection.

Now let's try for a final attempt to settle your account. If
you are unable to pay this amount, contact our office today to
arrange a repayment plan. Let's resolve this matter and return
your credit account to its former good standing.

Our toll-free number: 1-800-222-2222.

                                        F.B. Smith


PAST DUE: $532.18
```

DENIAL OF ADVERTISING REQUEST

SITUATION: The Junior Chamber of Commerce has asked XYZ Corporation to advertise in their Youth Salute Banquet program. Our budget prevents us from giving support.

Mr. Bob Brown
President
JUNIOR CHAMBER OF COMMERCE
123 Main Street
Somewhere, TX 75111

Your Youth Salute Banquet you put on each year helps recognize our youth. Thanks for taking the lead.

Because of our limited advertising budget, however, the request for advertising support in your Banquet Program must be denied.

Good luck with your banquet.

JOB DENIAL

SITUATION: David Scott has applied for an engineering job with XYZ Engineering. He's been invited for a second interview. Another who was also interviewed for a second time has been selected for the job. David Scott must be sent a letter informing him another has gotten the job.

Mr. David Scott
1111 N. Main Street
Fort Worth, TX 76107

Getting to know you has been a fine experience. Thank you for thinking of our company as a place where you would like to work.

Another person, however, has been selected for the engineering position. For this reason your application for employment must be denied.

When we visited I liked what I saw. I'm confident you should have little trouble finding a job. Good luck with your job search.

Ted E. Smith
Plant Manager

NO—SPEAKING ENGAGEMENT

SITUATION: John Smith has been asked to be the featured speaker at a Chamber of Commerce dinner on January 18. The dinner honors the "Man and Woman of the Year."

He will be unable to speak because of a prior commitment that requires him to be in Chicago on that day. He writes because he'd like to be considered again as a featured speaker.

Mr. Tom Jones
Chamber of Commerce
111 Main Street
Somewhere, TX 75111

It's an honor to be asked to speak at the Chamber's dinner for the "Man and Woman of the Year." What a special dinner.

If it were possible to be there, acceptance would be automatic. Because of a prior commitment in Chicago, however, I will be unable to attend the January 18 dinner. For this reason the speaking request must be turned down.

But I'd love a rain check to speak at a future meeting. The Chamber has given me so much. I'd like to return the favor.

Tom, I know your dinner will be a success. Good luck with it.

John Smith

MISSING AUTO POLICY FOR CAR LOAN

SITUATION: A loan customer has been asked to send a copy of his insurance policy to the bank to verify the bank as lienholder. No response has been received after two weeks.

This letter stresses the importance of the insurance coverage. It lets the loan customer save face by saying he might have put off sending the policy. It also points out the consequences of not sending the policy.

Your 1990 Ford pickup must have insurance coverage. And the coverage makes sense. It protects you in case of an emergency.

But we need your help on your insurance policy. Notice was sent to you, as we asked you to send us a copy of your insurance policy showing (name of bank) as lienholder. Neither a reply or the policy has been received. Often, in the hurry of everyday business, we put off some of our jobs. You could have done that with the policy.

Don't put off getting your policy to us any longer, however. Without proof of insurance, you're charged SINGLE INTEREST INSURANCE on the truck. The charge is tacked onto your loan. That insurance protects only the bank and its loan. It does not protect you.

And here's something else. SINGLE INTEREST INSURANCE is expensive. Let me repeat. It's expensive. Besides not protecting you, your car, and any liability you may incur, that insurance is often more than an individual insurance policy.

So get your insurance policy and proof of insurance to me by January 13. If you don't, SINGLE INTEREST INSURANCE charges kick in and are added to your loan. If you have questions, call me at 222-2222.

ORDER DELAY

SITUATION: A large department store has placed a rush order for five dozen sweaters. Twenty days have passed and a call has been made that the sweaters have not yet arrived.

Upon checking the order, we find that the sweaters were sent to the wrong retail store. A call has been made to the department store saying that a new shipment was sent by UPS the same day of the call. This letter aims at maintaining good will.

THEY'RE ON THE WAY, TOM:

In fact, you should have already received your sweater order.

After your telephone call, filling your order promptly was our number one priority. We sent your order UPS, and you should have received it the day after we talked.

Taking care of your needs is important to us. In the process, you helped us. Your original order was sent to another customer. We're changing our shipment procedures to ensure the kind of incident you experienced never happens again. Thanks for your help.

HAVE A GREAT CHRISTMAS SEASON . . .

OVERDRAFT THAT'S OVERDUE

SITUATION: A bank's customer has an overdraft of $161.40. A letter was sent asking for payment within two weeks. No payment was received. Now the bank is asking for payment again.

This letter stresses the importance of the credit rating and the consequences of a bad one. Notice that the salutation and the last paragraph tie in. And the last sentence is a call to action. You want payment. Ask for it. If nothing happens, then you do what you said you would do.

July 10, 1992

PROTECT YOUR CREDIT RATING:

Overdrafts are common in the banking industry. When they remain unpaid, however, that is uncommon. Pay the $161.40 overdraft from your account #1112234.

On June 25, 1992, a letter was sent to you asking you to pay the overdraft by July 9. No positive response has been received.

Either send payment to me by July 19 (specific date—10 days) or call me at 111-4444 by that date. If there are unusual circumstances, we'd like to know about them. We'll see if something can be worked out. But let us know what's happening.

If nothing is done, your account will be closed and the credit information will be reported to TRW, CheckSystem, and Checktronic. Your credit rating will be suspect and any loan will be difficult to obtain.

Yes, protect your credit. Drop your payment to us in the mail today.

(NO COMPLIMENTARY CLOSE.)

WRONG ORDER SENT

SITUATION: Twenty pen and pencil sets with the XYZ logo were ordered for an anniversary dinner and banquet. Twenty sets were received, but they had the wrong logo on them. The sets are to be given at a special recognition banquet for employees who have attained 30 years service.

A frantic Human Resources Manager has called you and asked that the correct pen and pencil sets be sent immediately. The correct order was sent by air express the day after the phone call. The pen and pencil sets will be received four days before the banquet.

OUCH! OUR FACES ARE RED, GEORGE:

Your pen and pencil sets with your company logo were sent air express the day after I received your call. You should have them in your hands by now.

How this mishap happened, I don't know. I do know, however, that I'm relieved that you have gotten the correct pen and pencil sets. Now you can recognize your people the way they should be.

As a long-standing customer, we'd like to recognize you too. Next time you order pen and pencil sets with your logo, give yourself a 50% discount for up to twenty. You deserve that special treatment.

HAVE A GREAT BANQUET . . .

P.S. When the dust settles, please ship those "surplus" pen and pencil sets to me by UPS collect. You certainly don't want them cluttering up your office.

THANK YOU FOR A CHARITABLE CONTRIBUTION

SITUATION: XYZ Corporation has been a continuous supporter for your medical charity. Because the gifts are large, a "thank you" note is a must.

The CEO of XYZ, Tom Adams, is a personal friend of the executive director of the foundation.

WHAT A DIFFERENCE YOU MAKE, TOM:

Your continuous help certainly gives us all a life. XYZ's check for 1999 of $100,000 is special. Thanks.

Your contribution makes the difference and gives us that extra that helps our research. We'd be unable to continue the cardiovascular study we're doing without your help.

It's a treat to count both XYZ and you as friends.

HAVE A TERRIFIC YEAR . . .

THANK YOU FOR POLITICAL CONTRIBUTION

SITUATION: A candidate for the United States House of Representatives thanks each contributor for contributions to the campaign.

YOUR SUPPORT STRENGTHENS OUR CAMPAIGN:

Your contribution in this campaign is what gives us an edge in our effort. You help us get our important message out. And that's rewarding for all of us who share the same beliefs. Thanks.

There's the old saying, "Put your money where your mouth is." You did just that.

But keep your voice going too. Let your friends and neighbors know what we are all about. Give them the satisfaction of knowing that they will have an effective Representative in Congress. Tell them, "John Hardy for Congress."

THANKS AGAIN . . .

THANK YOU FOR A HOLIDAY GIFT

SITUATION: A supplier of widgets has given you a shrimp platter as a way of saying thanks for your business.

The supplier has consistently given good service. The "thank you" is a way to strengthen the relationship.

YOU REALLY ARE SPECIAL, LONNIE:

That shrimp platter was terrific. My entire staff enjoyed it. Thanks for thinking of us.

Shortly after the platter arrived, my staff and I dove into the goodies. You really know how to pick us up. That shrimp platter just reconfirmed how much fun it is doing business with you.

HAVE A GREAT 1999!!!

THANK YOU FOR A REFERRAL

SITUATION: Bob Thomas referred Mary Smith to XYZ Corporation and let her use his name as a reference. She received the job and wants to thank Bob for his help.

YOUR HELP DID IT, BOB:

Looking for a new job is always tough. You made my search easy. Thanks for the referral.

I'm pleased to let you know I've accepted a job with XYZ Corporation and will start next week. I think your help made a difference in getting employed there.

I'll be moving to Oklahoma tomorrow. We'll be in different states, but let's stay in touch.

IT'S WONDERFUL COUNTING YOU AS A FRIEND

EMPLOYEE SUGGESTIONS

SITUATION: XYZ Company wants to start a company sponsored safety program to increase safety and safety awareness throughout its plant. To be successful, however, employee participation is a must.

GIVE YOURSELF A $500 BONUS . . .

. . . for making your workplace safer. Participate in the new Safety Program. And start today.

Since everyone at XYZ Company is a valuable part of our operation, we felt it was important to start a new Safety Program. That program is now in place.

Only you can make the Safety Program a success, however. To encourage participation in it, $500 will be given for each approved safety idea. Here's how the Safety Program works.

If you have a safety idea, write it out, sign it, and put it in one of the safety idea boxes located throughout the plant. A Safety Committee will then examine the merits of the suggestion.

That's when the rewards start. First, you get the opportunity to win $500 for yourself. Next, you'll have the satisfaction of knowing you contributed to making the workplace safer for you and your fellow workers. And last, you'll receive recognition.

Since only the safety committee reviews the ideas, the immediate supervisor never knows whether a safety idea has been submitted. That way possible friction between a supervisor and another employee is avoided.

The satisfaction you'll receive from your idea can be tremendous—"money," "improved safety," and "recognition." Everyone wins—you, your fellow workers, and your company.

So give yourself a bonus. Write out a suggestion and submit your idea for the Safety Program today.

HELP YOURSELF AND HELP OTHERS TOO . . .

P.S. If you have any questions about the new Safety Program, contact Fritz Howard in Human Resources at extension 1234. He'll be glad to help.

ASKING OTHERS TO ATTEND A MEETING

SITUATION: The organization NETWORK NETWORK has a monthly networking meeting with a featured speaker at each meeting. Maintaining interest is an ongoing challenge. Consequently, a persuasive letter is needed to encourage members to attend and to bring guests.

BE THERE AND GIVE YOURSELF A COMPETITIVE EDGE:

If you're looking for ideas to make a significant difference in your business, you won't want to miss our Saturday, April 13 networking meeting. Our speaker will be Bob Johnson, a time management expert who shows you how to save time so you can spend it more effectively.

Johnson, who specializes in the dynamics of time management, will present the program YOU DON'T SAVE TIME, YOU SPEND IT. He will challenge us to turn over a new leaf in how we use our time.

"You'll hear fresh ideas that will revolutionize how you handle your paper work, phone calls, and appointments," says NETWORK NETWORK organizer Warren Gather. "You'll learn how to get improved results using the time you have."

Author of YOU DON'T SAVE TIME, YOU SPEND IT, Johnson says that the approaches you hear will produce clear, bottom-line results. He'll share tips on how changing your habits impacts performance, promotability, and profits.

Johnson is president of his own consulting firm, Time Management Inc. He's worked with industry for over 15 years helping others help themselves.

Invest in your career and learn why and how time management gives you a step on the competition. Come hear him speak at the NETWORK NETWORK Saturday, April 13 meeting from 9:00am to noon at the Hawthorne Suites Hotel in Arlington. You'll be glad you did.

GIVE YOURSELF AN EDGE IN MANAGING TIME . . .

P.S. The cost is $10 at the door. But don't bring just yourself. Bring guests. Help them help themselves. For more information call (817)111-1111.

UNITED WAY FUND RAISING

SITUATION: Each fall the United Way appeals to the community to help it raise funds for worthwhile projects in the city. Part of that effort includes a letter that asks for support.

Notice in a fund raising letter that the request for funds is not in the first paragraph. No matter how rich someone is, they need time to become adjusted to wanting to give. So use a buffer paragraph.

YOU MAKE THE DIFFERENCE:

The best helping hand you have is at the end of your arm. But sometimes you need the helping hand of others. For instance, you go to a dentist for a tooth problem, a mechanic to fix your car, and a plumber to fix a water leak.

The United Way is also one of those other helping hands. We extend a helping hand to people throughout our community every day. Through 50 charitable organizations, we reach out and touch on a daily basis.

And that's why we need your help. So we can help others. Picture a Boy Scout earning a merit badge, a senior citizen receiving meals on wheels, or a wheelchair-ridden person using Handitran to get around. That's where your help goes, to help others help themselves.

Remember, every dollar of support for the United Way works harder. Because United Way is made up mostly of volunteers, 93% of each dollar contributed goes to support the individual agencies.

Use that helping hand you have at the end of your arm and help the United Way help others help themselves. Make a difference and give to the United Way. Put your contribution in the enclosed envelope and drop it in the mail. You'll be glad you did.

USE YOUR HELPING HAND . . .

P.S. Remember, your contribution is tax deductible. Yes, support the United Way.

SALVATION ARMY FUND RAISING

SITUATION: Massive layoffs in the community have created increased demand on the services of The Salvation Army. Without additional help from their regular contributors, services will have to be cut.

A special appeal is being made to prior contributors.

FIRST,
DAD LOST HIS JOB.
THEN HE LEFT HOME.
These are words we are hearing over and over again as people are being laid off.

NOBODY PLANS A LIFE FILLED WITH PROBLEMS . . .

sometimes it just happens.

That's the way it was with Sue. Her husband, Tom, lost his job. Feeling useless and unable to provide for his wife and three children, Tom abandoned them.

After losing their home, Sue and her children began living in a car. Then they heard of The Salvation Army's Family Center program and joined our program. FREE for up to ten weeks.

During their stay Sue began working her way back. While we took care of her children, she looked for work, found a job, and started saving money. These are the results we see time and again.

These uncertain times, however, have created a substantial increase in the demand to help others. While we are seeing more people asking for help, fewer are giving to us on a regular basis. Now we need your help again. We're in a precarious situation. Without further help, we'll have to cut some of our year-round programs.

This is not an ordinary appeal. We need help immediately. Without your support we'll be powerless to help others, because we'll have to cut back our services.

Your past support has helped us make a difference for those seeking help. Open your heart and give yourself the satisfaction of making a difference again. Join us in giving hope to others who desperately need help. Send your gift today.

GOD BLESS YOU . . .

P.S. Reach out and touch someone in need of help. Help The Salvation Army help those in need.

FOLLOW-UP TO ACQUIRE INSURANCE CUSTOMER

SITUATION: Jerry is not an insurance client of Gib. Gib, however, would like to become Jerry's agent. After obtaining motorcycle insurance for Jerry's sons, Gib uses this opportunity to plant a seed in Jerry's mind. That seed is that Gib should become Jerry's insurance agent.

The benefit of this kind of letter is not immediate. But what it does do is set the stage for things to come.

YOU HAVE A SPECIAL FAMILY, JERRY . . .

I enjoyed meeting Lance and Brett and was glad to help them with their motorcycle insurance.

Jerry, your business is important to me. I look forward to the opportunity of becoming your insurance agent and helping you with your Home, Auto, and Life insurance needs.

Count on me to provide the service your family wants and expects.

LET'S KEEP IN TOUCH,

Gib

MEMORANDUM THAT COMES TO POINT IMMEDIATELY

SITUATION: In writing a memorandum, the purpose must be identified immediately. The memo should not start with a "so what" thought. Rather, it should come to the point and let readers know first what is expected. This memorandum does just that.

January 30, 1999
TO: Mary Adams
            Don Peters
FROM: Tom Smith, Manager—Quality Control

SUBJECT: Meeting to discuss Laser Measurement Equipment, Z-103

To further examine the XYZ Company's Z-103, we'll have a meeting in my office at 10:00am on Monday, February 10, 1999. At the meeting we will discuss Z-103 merits and decide whether we want to purchase the equipment. To help you with a review of the Z-103 proposal, I've attached XYZ's proposal and promotional material.

To get a jump on the meeting discussion, please submit in writing your thoughts about XYZ's proposal by Friday, February 3, at 4:00pm. If unable to attend, let my secretary know on February 3 whom you will be sending in your place.

XYZ feels we'll improve the quality of _____ by converting to the Z-103. They say that our productivity will increase, that we'll have powerful quality control, and the end result will be even better customer satisfaction.

There are a number of advantages of converting to the Z-103. These three come to mind immediately. First, the laser equipment measures precision of ball screws, ball nuts, and ball screw/ball nut combinations to 0.00001 inch. Next, the software is easy to use. And last, the system is relatively insensitive to turbulence and can be used on the shop floor. You may have other comments.

We do expect some problems in converting to the Z-103. Conversion is expensive. The new equipment is expensive and costs $250,000. The conversion will interrupt three or more operations while people are learning the new system. You may have other comments here too.

MEMORANDUM WITH PARAGRAPH HEADLINING

SITUATION: To improve the effectiveness of a memorandum, use headlining. This approach uses summary words at the start of a paragraph that explain what the paragraph is all about. For added emphasis, those summary words are underlined.

The advantage of headlining is that it saves time for the busy executive, because it increases readability. With headlining the executive can see what's being discussed at a glance. He or she doesn't have to waste time plowing through the memorandum to find out what it's all about.

January 30, 1999

MEMORANDUM
TO: Mary Adams
         Don Peters
FROM: Tom Smith, Manager—Quality Control
SUBJECT: Meeting to discuss Laser Measurement Equipment, Z-103

Meeting Announcement: To further examine the XYZ Company's Z-103, we'll have a meeting in my office at 10:00am on Monday, February 10, 1999.

Purpose of Meeting: We will discuss Z-103 merits and decide whether we want to purchase the equipment. To help you with a review of the Z-103 proposal, I've attached XYZ's proposal and promotional material.

Actions Requested: To get a jump on the meeting discussion, please submit in writing your thoughts about XYZ's proposal by Friday, February 3 at 4:00pm. If unable to attend the meeting, let my secretary know on February 3 whom you will be sending in your place.

XYZ's Views of the Benefits: XYZ feels we'll improve the quality of _____ by converting to the Z-103. They say that our productivity will increase, that we'll have powerful quality control, and the end result will be even better customer satisfaction.

Advantages: There are a number of advantages of converting to the Z-103. These three come to my mind immediately. First, the laser equipment measures precision of ball screws, ball nuts, and ball screw/ball nut combinations to 0.00001 inch. Next, the software is easy to use. And last, the system is relatively insensitive to turbulence and can be used on the show floor. You may have other comments.

Disadvantages: We do expect some problems in converting to the Z-103. Conversion is expensive. The new equipment is expensive and costs $250,000. The conversion will interrupt three or more operations while people are learning the new system. You may have other comments here, too.

ANNOUNCING A NEW LOCATION

SITUATION: The XYZ Laser Copy store has outgrown its present location and moved to a bigger store. It wants to let customers and clients know that they moved. They also want to share their good fortune of growing.

This letter announces the news and encourages customers to come and use the services at the new store.

WE'RE MOVING!!!

It's official. Next Monday, July 7, we'll be at a new and larger location, 111 Cooper Street, across from the Parks Mall.

That new store comes because of one reason — customers like you. You've used our services. Thanks for your support and faith in us.

Now we'd like to recognize that support. Bring this letter with you next time you're in need of our services. You'll get a 15% discount on anything we sell or offer. It's our way of saying thanks.

COME SEE US AND GET A 15% DISCOUNT!!!

APPRECIATION FOR PAST SUPPORT

SITUATION: XYZ GRAPHICS recognizes the importance of expressing appreciation to long-standing customers. They want to acknowledge the fine relationship they've had over the years.

This letter is to reinforce that long-standing relationship.

THANKS FOR A WINNING RELATIONSHIP, TOM:

Filling your needs and working with you is like scoring a touchdown or hitting a home run. That relationship is a winner.

We've been supplying your graphic needs for ten years. You've expected quality work from us. Your coming back is a vote of confidence in the job we've been doing for you. Thanks for that vote.

We are looking forward to working with you on future projects and continuing the kind of service your company expects and deserves. Tom, it's good doing business with you.

HAVE A PROFITABLE 1999 . . .

LOOKING FOR A PUBLISHING AGENT

SITUATION: Aspiring authors need an agent to help them get their books published. A letter asking for an agent to take a look must be hard hitting and show why the book will be of interest. This letter is for a "how to" book.

The letter uses the "Sales Plan" to get its message across. The "creative substitution" creates interest in the salutation and adds a selling thought at the end.

WHY TAKE ME ON AS A CLIENT?

That's easy. Your agency will be taking on a client with a money making book, <u>You Don't Save Time, You Spend It Efficiently</u>, that will impact industry habits on managing time.

Here's why industry will want the book. Their employees will learn:

— how to change paper work habits to free them for more productive work,

— how to handle telephone calls more efficiently so the calls don't interrupt but rather work for them,

— how to schedule appointments so time works as a negotiating tool.

To show you my approach, I've attached an article, "Using Time to Negotiate," from WIDGET WORLD, the official publication of the National Widget Association. A member who read the article called me from New York and said, "Your ideas have already helped me in my business. I can't wait for you to write another article for us."

Now for some information about me. It's enclosed and includes:

— a biographical sketch that supports my time management credentials

— a magazine article, "How to Spend Time and Make Money,"

— three testimonials.

Let me know when you're interested. Use the courtesy envelope and say, Let's have some more." We'll both win.

TIME MEANS MONEY,

ASKING FOR AN EXTENSION OF TIME FOR A BOOK CONTRACT

SITUATION: Writing a book requires contract deadlines by the author. Sometimes delays cause the author to need added time. Here's a letter that asks for that time.

SUBJECT: BUSINESS LETTERS THAT GET RESULTS

I NEED MORE TIME, BRANDON:

I'm not looking at months or a month. I'm looking to extend my contract deadline to January 31.

The book has taken more time to prepare than I anticipated. Most of it is finished but requires refinement. You asked for a January 15 deadline. I need until January 31.

When you were considering my book, you asked for examples. You saw some. Here are two others that show how the ideas in the book are developing. The first has a bank asking customers to establish a line of credit. The other explains a delayed order.

I wish I had the entire book done today. But I will get it to you shortly.

WRITE POWERFULLY . . .

ASKING FOR CREDIT CARD APPLICATION

SITUATION: Credit card companies consistently send out letters asking potential users to enroll with their credit card. This letter uses techniques of the "Sales Plan" to encourage acceptance of the application.

YOU'VE GOT IT, MR. JONES . . .

. . . YOU'VE BEEN PRE-APPROVED!!!

Few have the credit reputation you carry. And even fewer are approved for the _____ gold membership privileges. You're invited to join an extraordinary circle of executives and professionals.

Because I believe you are a person who will appreciate this valuable and prestigious financial instrument, come aboard and take advantage of what the _____ Gold Card offers.

<u>The _____ Gold Card is</u>

<u>pre-approved in your name.</u>

Yes, you are one of a select few who automatically meets our rigorous standards for Gold Card membership. <u>Your acceptance is assured.</u>

Carrying the _____ Gold Card affords you instant recognition and unquestioned credit worldwide. Picture what you have at your fingertips — fine restaurants and stores, hotels and resorts, and airline tickets to business and vacation spots throughout the world.

And there's more. Expect an unparalleled level of personal service 24 hours a day that includes worldwide travel benefits, emergency assistance, and financial advantages other cards simply don't give you—for only $_____ a year.

So take advantage of what the _____ Gold Card offers. Join us today. While you are thinking about it, fill out the enrollment form below and return it by the date shown. <u>We'll dash your _____ Gold Card to you immediately.</u>

CAPTURE THE EXCELLENCE OF _____ . . .

P.S. An offer of Pre-approved Gold Card membership says a lot about you. Congratulations.

BANKING—HOME IMPROVEMENT LOAN

SITUATION: May 1, the (name of bank) sends out a letter to its customers encouraging them to take out home improvement loans. To make the effort easier, the bank waives closing costs on loans up to $25,000 and gives a lower interest rate for automatic withdrawal from an account.

NOW YOU SAVE THREE WAYS ON . . .

(NAME OF BANK) HOME IMPROVEMENT LOANS

If you've been thinking about improving your home—either inside or out—now's the time. (name of bank) customer can save three ways:

— Low fixed interest rates!

— No closing costs on loans up to $25,000!

— 100% tax-deductible interest!

First, not only are the fixed rates competitive, you can get an even lower rate when you arrange to have your monthly payment made automatically from a (name of bank) account.

Next, for a limited time we are waiving all closing costs on loans up to $25,000. This averages $200-$300 in savings. So it's certainly worth the effort to explore this opportunity today.

And last, the loan is tax deductible. Current tax laws permit you to deduct interest on your (name of bank) Home Improvement Loan. One nice feature is you can get the loan for what you want: a hot tub, a bath, a remodeled kitchen. Consult your tax advisor for details.

Perhaps the best news is how easy it is to get a (name of bank) Home Improvement Loan. To get started, just bring in the enclosed Certificate of Value to your nearest (name of bank) branch before July 31, 1992. There's no waiting around. You'll have your answer within two business days after your application.

Give yourself the satisfaction of both improving your home and saving money. Apply for a (name of bank) Home Improvement Loan today.

ENJOY HOME IMPROVEMENTS TODAY!!!

P.S. Take advantage of this special opportunity. The phone number and address of your nearest (name of bank) branch appear on the enclosed Certificate of Value. Call or visit today. You'll like your decision.

WELCOMING A NEW BANK CUSTOMER

SITUATION: After customers open their first account with XYZ Bank, a letter is sent out that welcomes them to the bank. In addition, you use this letter to further acquaint them with some of the services you offer and to encourage them to take advantage of them.

WELCOME TO XYZ BANKING, MR. JONES:

As a member of the family of customers at XYZ, you'll find a wealth of services available to you. You've opened both check and savings accounts. These are just two of the services you can expect.

If you want to generate interest, take a look at our IRAs and certificates of deposit. If you need a car or home improvement loan, let us know. If you want travelers checks, transfer of funds, or a credit card, we can help.

As you use our three convenient locations, you'll discover a friendly touch. Tellers, loan officers, and other banking people will share their enthusiasm to have you as part of the XYZ family.

To give you a better picture of what we offer, enclosed are brochures about some of the XYZ services you can take advantage of. Examine them. You may not need the services now, but you will be knowledgeable on what is available.

For prompt, individual attention about the special financial services we offer, visit any of our locations and talk to our banking experts. They'll provide you with the personal banking you expect.

WE'RE GLAD TO HAVE YOU WITH US . . .

LETTER AFTER INITIAL PHONE CALL

SITUATION: After a telephone call inquiring about the timing of XYZ Association's next convention, a letter and informational packet are sent. This cover letter is a sales letter that creates rapport with the "creative substitution." In addition, the letter creates an air of curiosity by painting a picture of benefits.

YOU'LL LIKE WHAT WE HAVE TO OFFER, TOM:

As I said on the phone, if you're looking to put together a powerful convention for the XYZ Association, Dallas delivers. Enclosed is an informational packet that discusses what you will receive.

First, expect excellent facilities that will meet your specifications. You'll find ample rooms available, extensive meeting space, an option of many visitor attractions, splendid shopping, and excellent restaurants.

Next, you can expect meeting expertise that helps you create a smooth convention. For instance, the Convention and Visitors Bureau helps you with a vast range of services. Some include:

- providing a survey of hotel and meeting facilities,

- counseling on development of programs,

- planning activities for both members and spouses.

And last, you'll find that our convention class hotels want to cater to your needs. They know the importance of making your convention a success. Expect to be pampered.

Dallas and its Convention & Visitors bureau would be honored to host your convention in 1999. Yes, Tom, select Dallas for a first class convention. You'll like your choice.

DISTINCTIVELY DALLAS

Sales Manager

P.S. For more information and for solutions, I'm just a phone call away. Call me at (214)000-0000.

CONVENTION CENTER RESPONSE TO A POSITIVE DECISION

SITUATION: The XYZ Association wrote you that they have chosen Dallas for their next convention site. You want to reinforce their decision.

YOU'LL LIKE YOUR DECISION, MS. _____:

You'll find that selecting Dallas as your site for your next convention is a good one. You can expect these benefits:

— excellent facilities to handle your specs and requirements,

— hotel people who will help you run a smooth and successful convention,

— a staff at the Convention Center who will help the (name of association or company) put together the best convention ever.

As soon as you told us of your selection, we sent a letter to area hotels. They should be in touch with you within ten days. The letter to them is attached.

For your information, I'm sending you the "Dallas 1999 Planner." After reviewing it, I think you'll see it's a wonderful resources for information about our fine city. For additional information, call me directly at 214-000-0000. I'm just a phone call away.

Dallas will meet your members' needs, Sue. I look forward to working with you and your staff for your convention.

COUNT ON US TO HELP . . .

Sales Manager

P.S. We're honored to have your fine (prestigious) organization, _____, select Dallas as its convention site. Expect a successful convention.

HOTEL HOPING TO CAPTURE CONVENTION BUSINESS

SITUATION: The XYZ Association has informed the Dallas Convention Center that they will hold their 1999 convention in Dallas. Hotels have been contacted and asked to get in touch with the Association.

Your hotel wants XYZ members to use its facility. You send the association information and say you will follow-up with a call.

WELCOME, MS. SMITH . . .

. . . to the excitement of Dallas and the wealth of activities available to your members. It's a city that offers what you expect.

Now that you know you will be here, let us help you capture Dallas's exciting flavor. Take advantage of our convention class facilities that will meet your specifications. Take advantage of our convenient location minutes from the Convention Center. And take advantage of our meeting expertise that will help insure a smooth convention.

To give you information on what we offer and what it will cost, I've enclosed our "Convention Packet." Examine it. You'll find many benefit that will help you help your members.

Ms. Smith, take advantage of the service you expect and receive from our people. Stay at the _____ Hotel. You'll be glad you did.

I'll call you <u>Tuesday, May 3,</u> to see how we can meet your needs.

LET US HELP MAKE YOUR CONVENTION A SUCCESS

Sales Manager

P.S. We don't knock the competition. We beat them. Yes, you'll like what you find at _____ Hotel.

SENDING REQUESTED INFORMATION

SITUATION: XYZ puts an ad in each Tuesday Business Section of the "Dallas Morning News" and encourages companies and individuals to call and ask for information about its computer training programs.

After an initial call this cover letter accompanies the information and sells the idea of participating in the training at the same time.

HERE'S THE TRAINING INFORMATION, MR. SMITH:

Enclosed is the XYZ course information and schedule you requested. Thanks for your interest in our Lotus 1-2-3 release 2.2 courses.

Whether you're looking for computer training for yourself or for your people, we can help. As a Lotus, Borland, Ashton-Tate, Xerox, and Microrim Authorized Training Center, XYZ has established itself as a leader in the field of training and support. Currently our 43 locations across the country train over 10,000 people each month.

XYZ of Texas offers classes daily in our training center on LBJ Freeway. The cost for each one day course is $195 (except for desktop publishing classes which are $225) and includes:

* professional instruction from full time trainers,

* manual and practice diskette to keep for future reference,

* <u>free</u> continuing telephone support about course material,

* "hands on" learning with each person working individually at a PC,

* maximum of 10-12 student in a class.

We also offer a special Annual Membership for $795. For a full year an Annual Member is entitled to attend an <u>unlimited</u> number of classes scheduled on our monthly update calendar. This includes all of our desktop publishing and two-day advanced classes.

Give me a call at (214)111-1111 to register for a course or for further information. You'll be glad you did.

GIVE YOURSELF AN EDGE WITH XYZ TRAINING . . .

ENCOURAGING OTHERS TO JOIN A DENTAL PLAN

SITUATION: The Consumers' Association for Professional Services offer a dental plan with reduced dental costs. The Association was formed to provide quality professional services at affordable rates.

This letter is sent out after a prospective plan member calls a number listed in the yellow pages. The Association is a member of the Better Business Bureau.

CAPS

Consumers' Association for Professional Services

HEALTHIER TEETH FOR LESS MONEY:

That's right. You can save money while receiving excellent dental care. You'll smile at these benefits:

* Save 20% to 50% on each visit to the dentist

* Professional care by qualified dentists

* No waiting period, benefits effective immediately

* Low annual family membership $74.00 (individual membership $44.00)

* Two FREE check-ups a year for each family member

A smile that glistens with good health sends a powerful message. Read the enclosed circular and discover how to keep that smile while you're saving money.

You'll not only get reduced dental fees, but there are no deductibles, no restrictions, no limitations, no waiting period, and no exclusions for pre-existing conditions. Translation: without a deductible, your benefits begin immediately.

Start your reduced dental services today. Fill out the enrollment application and drop it in the mail. You'll be glad you did.

SMILE WITH OUR PLAN!

P.S. The sooner you send in your check, the sooner your benefits begin.

DIRECT MAIL

SITUATION: A small advertising firm is being aggressive in a recession. They are sending a direct mail piece to members of the local Chamber of Commerce.

The letter gets the attention. The inserts, not included with this letter, capture the interest.

GIVE YOURSELF AN EDGE:

We've decided to boycott the recession. How about you?

While some firms maintain a low profile during tough times, smart businesses think smart. They promote themselves and grow as a result.

<u>Shoestring Advertising</u> can help you be one of those smart businesses. And at a price that makes sense. Simply put, we offer the marketing insight and high quality you expect to find with a large ad agency or graphics firm, but at far less cost.

Examine the enclosed samples of our work and our mission sheet on value. You'll like what you see. Then say, "I'd like to know more about growing on a limited budget." For that information, call me at <u>(202)111-1111</u>. You'll be glad you made that call.

LET'S GET OPTIMISTIC

Fred F. Smith

President

INSURANCE—Proposal for Company

SITUATION: The XYZ Insurance Company sends a letter to small companies to get them interested in an insurance plan and annuity that acts as a benefit plan for employees. The letter is directed at companies ranging in size from 50 to 250.

GIVE YOUR EMPLOYEES A NEW BENEFIT PLAN AT NO COST TO YOU,
_____:

Imagine a new employee benefit for your company that costs you nothing. Sound far fetched? It's not.

We're offering a new concept in corporate life insurance and retirement benefits, SECURITY PLUS. With no cost to you, employees choose whether to enroll in this voluntary benefit program.

By enrolling employees can expect these benefits:

- guaranteed retirement values 2 to 3 times larger than an ordinary annuity,

- disability payments,

- life insurance protection,

- coverage for the entire family,

- a portable plan that requires no vesting.

And how do employees receive this program? They like it. Participation is high, because employees perceive the program as a company benefit. Your only involvement would be to provide employees time to meet with an enrollment counselor and provide premium payments through payroll deduction.

Give your company an added benefit <u>without the expense</u> of an added benefit. Examine the enclosed information and tell yourself, "I like what I see." Then to find out more about the benefit plan, complete and return the enclosed courtesy card. You'll be glad you did.

GIVE YOUR COMPANY A NEW BENEFIT PLAN . . .
Gordon Field
Representative

P.S. To get faster service, call me at <u>(817) 111-1111</u>.

INSURANCE—New Benefit Plan for Employees

SITUATION: XYZ Corporation had decided to make available an insurance and annuity plan for its employees. At no cost to the company, XYZ is offering a voluntary employee benefit plan to its employees. To make employees aware of the plan, a letter is being sent to them. It encourages them to participate.

TO ALL (COMPANY NAME) EMPLOYEES:

We like it. After reviewing an employee benefit program, we feel it has exceptional benefits for each of you. Consequently, we are making it available through the company for you and your family.

This program, called Security PLUS, will give every employee an opportunity to supplement current insurance with a new and unique insurance plan. It's unique because it couples life insurance with exceptional Retirement Values.

The Retirement Values are exceptional, because they are usually 2 to 3 times larger than similar plans. What does that mean for you? You can expect an 11% to 16% return on your money. And that includes life insurance.

As evidence of our faith in the plan, we are making participation easy. You can participate on a voluntary basis through the convenience of payroll deduction.

Keep in mind this plan is not intended to replace your existing group life and retirement benefits. Rather, it is designed to supplement and strengthen them. There's one other feature. Should you ever terminate employment, there are no vesting requirements. You can take this plan with you without loss of benefits or a cost increase.

(Company name) adopted this program with you and your family in mind. As such, we made arrangements to have the plan personally explained to each of you. You will be notified of the exact time and location for your individual interview.

After personally reviewing this unique program, I urge each of you to give this plan serious consideration before accepting or rejecting it. You'll be glad you did.

After enrolling, except for payroll deduction of premium payments, all your contacts are with the firm representing _____ Insurance Company, not (company name).

I'm glad we can offer the program to you.
Name
Title

INSURANCE—Proposal to Professionals for Annuity

SITUATION: An insurance agent sends out a direct mail piece to doctors to encourage them to supplement their current retirement plans. Annuities are often considered dull. This letter adds a new selling approach for them.

MAKE UNCLE SAM EARN HIS OWN MONEY, DR. ANDERSON:

When you are in a higher tax bracket, it's imperative that you accumulate wealth with as little interference as possible. Why make Uncle Sam a silent partner who shares your profits? You don't have to.

We have a retirement program that not only provides TAX-FREE income, but also makes that income available whenever you want it — with minimum tax consequences and WITHOUT PENALTY.

And there are other advantages that free you from government regulations:

- no IRS approval required compared to a qualified plan and requires no annual administrative cost,

- unlike qualified plans and Keogh plans, gives tax free access to accumulated cash in the plan that let's you use the cash any way you want,

- not subject to annual ERISA reporting requirements,

- tax advantages let you fund your retirement plan with less money and receive tax free distributions as much as 60% higher,

- includes substantial Life Insurance at no added cost.

Find out more about this money-saving retirement plan that divorces itself from Uncle Sam. Just complete and return the enclosed courtesy card. Or for faster information, call me at (817) 111-1111. You'll be glad you did.

LET UNCLE SAM BE SOMEONE ELSE'S PARTNER . . .
Gordon Field
Representative

P.S. The sooner you act, the sooner you can accumulate money for your retirement, TAX FREE.

INVITATION TO ATTEND A CONVENTION

SITUATION: Each May the International Speakers Association sends an invitation to all members to attend its July International Convention. This letter is from the organization's president and stresses career investment.

IT'S AN INVESTMENT IN YOUR SPEAKING CAREER!!!

Mark July 18 to July 23 on your calendar and plan to attend the International Speakers Association International Convention. You'll hear practical ideas and successful techniques that will accelerate your career. And you'll be able to put the ideas to work immediately.

With 50 educational sessions scheduled, you'll find a variety of career-building programs that address your needs. Whether you are an aspiring or developing speaker or a seasoned pro, you'll discover exciting sessions. For instance, given the number of excellent sessions available, you can expect programs like this:

— THE GENIUS OF GREAT AUDIENCE PARTICIPATION

— HOW TO SUCCESSFULLY WORK WITH SPEAKERS BUREAUS AND INCREASE YOUR BOOKINGS

— BUILDING YOUR SPEAKING BUSINESS FROM POINT ZERO TO FAME AND FORTUNE

Make the decision today to take advantage of the valuable opportunity our International Convention offers. Fill out the enclosed registration form and mail it to the ISA office in Dallas. Completing and returning that form will be one of the most important investments you'll ever make in your career.

SEE YOU IN LONDON . . .

REQUESTING CORPORATE SUPPORT FOR PROFESSIONAL ASSOCIATION

SITUATION: Each October the Dallas Chapter of the National Secretaries Association puts on a seminar for its members. To have quality speakers and facilities, the local chapter members ask for corporate support from their bosses.

Barbara Smith of XYZ Corporation has asked her boss's boss for support from XYZ.

```
TO:      Robert Hall
FROM:    Barbara Smith
SUBJECT: NSA Secretarial Seminar
```

I recommend that XYZ Corporation provide financial support of $500 for the upcoming NSA Secretarial Seminar.

Value to the Company: Any training received reflects on the professionalism of the secretary and the quality of performance she provides her boss. Her exposure to new ideas benefits her, her boss, and XYZ Corporation.

Upcoming Training: Each year the Dallas Chapter of NSA hosts an annual secretarial seminar to help secretaries improve their skills. Five of our secretaries are members of NSA and will attend. Continuing education like that being offered improves the success of both the secretary and executive.

Corporate Support Is Needed: Cost is always a struggle for a nonprofit organization. To help ease the expense and enable us to have an effective seminar, corporate contributions are being sought. I recommend that XYZ Corporation donate $500 to the Dallas Chapter of NSA to help create a career-building seminar.

Seminar Date: The seminar is scheduled for Saturday, October 20. So secretaries can attend without interrupting company operations, we scheduled it on a weekend.

The Speakers: We have two exciting and powerful speakers. Their presentations will help those attending learn ideas to help them help their bosses. One is Jay Jones, Business Letters Unlimited, who will present REVOLUTIONIZE YOUR WRITING. The other, Anita Reed of Anita Reed Seminars, will present a program called EVERY WORKING WOMAN NEEDS A WIFE! (flyers attached).

Should you required added information, call me at 1111.

RETAIL STORE INVITATION TO COLLEGE STUDENTS TO ACQUIRE CREDIT CARD

SITUATION: Before each fall semester, (name of store) Department Store sends letters to college seniors that invite them to become credit-card holders.

For ease of response a courtesy envelope is enclosed for the student to return the application.

IT'S AN INVITATION TO SAY "CHARGE IT":

As you prepare to return the campus or start on your new career, (name of store) invites you to enjoy the convenience of a (name of store) charge account. And that convenience means you'll have immediate access to our vast selection of merchandise.

For campus activities and upcoming interviews, you'll probably want to expand your wardrobe to look your best. We can help you do that. With our quality fashions, you can expect to find clothes that will help you "dress for success." All you have to do is say, "CHARGE IT."

Furnishing a new apartment can also be a challenge. We can help you meet that challenge. You'll find all the basics you need to survive in your first home. From kitchen housewares to towels and linens, all you'll have to do is say, "CHARGE IT."

And there's another benefit. Using your new (name of store) credit card wisely will help you establish a credit record which will prove invaluable in future years.

Take advantage of our offer and acquire a (name of store) credit card. Take a moment to complete and mail the application today. You'll be glad you did.

GIVE YOURSELF CREDIT!!!

P.S. We look forward to serving you often in the years ahead.

RECOMMENDATION OF FORMER EMPLOYEE: Salesperson

SITUATION: Tom Johnson has worked for ten years for XYZ Company and has developed an outstanding reputation. He wants a letter of recommendation because he is moving to a different city.

This letter breaks tradition and creates interest in both the salutation and complimentary close with "creative substitutions."

WARNING: "To Whom It May Concern" is a "no no."

GRAB HIM. HE'S GOOD!!!

Tom Johnson was under my direct supervision for ten years. His performance with me was spectacular.

Each year he improved his sales results. And each year he exceeded quotas established for those in his sales team. Yes, he was an outstanding performer.

What made him special was how he consistently added new customers. He was always going that extra mile to see who else he could help.

I'll miss him and his cheerful approach toward work. He always said he wanted to be the best he could be. And he was. I sure wish he would have stayed.

EXPECT RESULTS WITH TOM JOHNSON . . .

RECOMMENDATION OF FORMER EMPLOYEE: Secretary

SITUATION: Mary Brad is moving with her husband to another city where he was transferred. She's worked for you for three years and has been a terrific asset to you. She asks for a letter of recommendation.

GIVE YOURSELF A WINNER WITH MARY BRAD:

If you're looking for a dependable secretary who consistently makes you look good, then Mary Brad is for you.

For three years she was my personal secretary. She was outstanding.

She wasn't someone who just had good secretarial skills. She was a contributor. She was my sounding board. I also encouraged her to give me ideas, and she did. Those ideas of hers helped improve my performance.

And she has another valuable talent. She's an excellent writer. Frequently she drafted letters for my signature. That was a time saver.

Yes, Mary Brad will do a first class job for you. I wish she were staying.

YOU'LL LIKE WHAT SHE HAS TO CONTRIBUTE . . .

REMOVAL OF UNAUTHORIZED CREDIT CARD CHARGES

SITUATION: A credit card company has billed us for an unauthorized charge of $20.00 for a HOTLINE CREDIT CARD SERVICE. We want the charge dropped.

The tone is friendly but firm. Notice that the letter starts with the friendly, "I NEED YOUR HELP." Use this language when you expect no difficulty with settlement.

I NEED YOUR HELP: ACCOUNT: 111 111 111 111

My experience with you says "A+." Now transfer some of that "A+" to my account. Credit it for $20.

There must have been some computer mistake. I did not order your HOTLINE CREDIT CARD SERVICE yet I was billed for it. How I received it, I don't know. But I did. Due process requires notice. I received none about the HOTLINE CREDIT CARD SERVICE. I should have.

My credit history shows that I pay my bills promptly. If I owed the $20, I'd be glad to pay it. But I won't.

Some computer foul-up must have caused the billing for the HOTLINE LOST CARD SERVICE. Crank up your computer so it credits my account for $20.00.

Jay Jones

FOLLOW-UP IRS

SITUATION: When you submitted your 1999 tax form, you indicated you were entitled to a refund of $1,222. The IRS now says you owe money. For your personal return you accidentally indicated a profit from your business when in fact it should have been a loss (Schedule C).

The IRS wrote you and asked you for more taxes, $5,100. You answered and explained the mistake and again asked for your refund.

DARN IT! IT'S MY GOVERNMENT TOO:

Yes, if we owe taxes we should pay them. As citizens we have a responsibility to pay our taxes. But I don't owe taxes and am, in fact, entitled to the $1,222 refund I asked for originally. <u>Send me a refund check for $1,222.</u>

When I submitted my 1999 tax return I inadvertently listed my 1999 business loss as a gain. That explains why you indicate I owe you additional taxes.

To show you why I'm entitled to the refund, I've attached copies of my 1040 (A) and Schedule C (B). Both forms indicate a profit from my business. That explains why you indicate I owe $5,100 in taxes. But that's not right.

Examine my Schedule C, and you'll find that I had a loss, not a gain. My only mistake was that I failed to put the loss in brackets. Consequently, both the 1040 and Schedule C suggest a gain. That's wrong.

Take out your pencil and recalculate the taxes. You'll see that I am entitled to a $1,222 refund. <u>Then send me a check for that amount.</u>

                              Robert Y. Taxpayer

FOLLOW-UP Service Delay

SITUATION The XYZ Printing Company supplies us with all our printing needs from letterhead and business cards to annual reports and colored promotional items. Their quality is excellent.

Recently, however, the company has been late in getting our four-colored printed matter to us. A recent delay caused us to postpone a direct mail campaign. This is unacceptable. We're writing to let XYZ know we expect timely delivery.

IT'S GOT TO STOP:

Your quality of printing is outstanding. Delivery of that printing is not. We expect our printing orders to be on time.

Recently our orders have been delivered to us from two to five days later than the time promised. This practice has got to stop.

Let's look at our relationship. It's been rewarding for both of us. We receive outstanding service coupled with a terrific dose of creativity. For instance, with the widget promotion you helped us develop the color theme for our marketing program. We liked that.

In return for your quality work, we've given all our business to you. Now that relationship is in jeopardy because of your untimely delivery of printing orders.

We know you can meet deadlines. Do.

We've talked to you about these delays, but nothing seemed to come of those talks. That's why I'm writing. Let this letter stand as notice that we are continuing our business with you on a trial basis only. If printing deadlines are not met, we will find another supplier.

Tom, we've been good for each other. Let's keep it that way. Get our printing requirements to us on time.

F.F. Furman

P.S. Call me. Let's clear the air.

WRONG ORDER SENT

SITUATION: A sporting goods store ordered three dozen Green Bay Packer sweat-shirts with matching sweatpants. The color was incorrect. It was "Kelly Green" rather than the ordered "Forest Green." In addition, the sweat-shirts and sweatpants were of different textures. The order was unacceptable.

The XYZ salesperson has indicated that XYZ would send a "return voucher authorization" so the sweats could be returned and the sporting goods store would get credit for these items.

LET'S GET THIS STRAIGHTENED OUT:

When it's broken, fix it. When it's bent, straighten it out. Our order #12345 is bent. Straighten it out and <u>send us a "return voucher authorization."</u>

On September 17, we received three dozen Green Bay Packer sweatshirts and three dozen sweatpants for order #12345. They were not, however, what we ordered. We ordered "Forest Green." The sweatshirts and sweatpants we received were "Kelly Green," a significant different in color.

In addition, the sweatshirts and sweatpants did not match because they had different fabric textures.

Because of the color and texture differences, order #12345 is unacceptable.

On September 18, I talked to you on the phone about this mix-up and also sent you a copy of our order #12345 and your invoice. Your invoice clearly shows a discrepancy from what we actually ordered.

You indicated you'd straighten this matter out and send us a "return voucher authorization," so we could have our account credited for the merchandise. Thirty-five days have passed since we talked and still no "return voucher authorization." We should have received it.

To support the mix-up, I'm again sending you copies of order #12345 (enclosure 1) and your invoice for that order (enclosure 2).

Examine them and say, "I agree. The situation needs a solution." Then straighten out this merchandise mix-up. <u>Send us the "return voucher authorization" for order #12345 today so we can return the merchandise and get credit for it.</u>

David S. Jones

NOTES

Chapter 2 — The Salutation and Complimentary Close—Do We Need Them?

1. Poe, Roy W., *The McGraw-Hill Handbook of Business Letters*, 2nd Edition, McGraw-Hill Book Company: New York, 1988, p. 34.

2. Wertz, Edward W., *Letters That Sell*, 2nd Edition, Contemporary Books, Inc.: Chicago, 1987, p. 155.

3. Sabin, William A., *The Gregg Reference Manual*, 5th Edition, Gregg Division/McGraw-Hill: New York, 1977, p. 254.

4. Frailey, L.E., *Handbook of Business Letters*, 3rd Edition, Prentice Hall: Englewood Cliffs, NJ, 1989, p. 217.

Chapter 4 — The "Yes" Plan

1. Kenneth Blanchard, Ph.D., Spencer Johnson, M.D., *The One Minute Manager*, Berkley Books: New York, 1982, p. 39.

Chapter 5 — The "No" Plan

1. Aurner, Robert R., *Effective Communications in Business*, 4th Edition, South-Western Publishing Co.: New Rochelle, NY, 1958, p. 433.

2. Ibid., p. 433

3. Ibid., p. 433

4. Bolander, Donald O. and Madeline Semmelmeyer, *Instant English Handbook*, Revised Edition, Career Publishing Co.: Little Falls, NJ, 1984, p. 173.

5. Ibid., p. 166.

Chapter 7 — Persuading Tips that Get Results

1. Communication and Leadership Program, Toastmasters International Inc.: Santa Ana, CA, 1977, p. 31.

Chapter 8 — The Sales Plan, The Home Run

1. Kremer, John, *Mail Order Selling Made Easy*, Ad-Lib Publications: Fairfield, IA, 1990, p. 63.

2. Wertz, Edward W., *Letters That Sell*, 2nd Edition, Contemporary Books, Inc.: Chicago, 1987, p. 155.

3. Wertz, ibid., p. 8.

4. Kremer, ibid.

5. Meyer, Harold E., *Lifetime Encyclopedia of Letters*, Prentice-Hall: Englewood Cliffs, NJ, 1983, p. 85.

6. Hoke, Henry, "How to Think About Writing Direct Mail Letters," *Fund Raising Management*, March-April 1970, p. 32.

7. Gnam, Rene, "New Direct Mail Techniques for Speakers," Speech at National Speakers Association National Convention, Nashville, TN, July 11, 1987.

8. Gnam, ibid.

9. Kremer, ibid., p. 65.

10. Kremer, ibid., p. 66.

11. Kremer, ibid., p. 66.

12. Katzenstein, Herbert, *Direct Marketing*, Charles E. Merrill Publishing Company: Columbus, 1986, p. 240.

INDEX OF LETTERS